Part 5 Digital freedom: the good, the bad and the internet

You can find this part of the block online. A link is provided on the TU100 website.

The Open University

TU100
My digital life

Block 5
My society

This publication forms part of the Open University module TU100 *My digital life*. Details of this and other Open University modules can be obtained from the Student Registration and Enquiry Service, The Open University, PO Box 197, Milton Keynes MK7 6BJ, United Kingdom (tel. +44 (0)845 300 60 90; email general-enquiries@open.ac.uk).

Alternatively, you may visit the Open University website at www.open.ac.uk where you can learn more about the wide range of modules and packs offered at all levels by The Open University.

To purchase a selection of Open University materials visit www.ouw.co.uk, or contact Open University Worldwide, Walton Hall, Milton Keynes MK7 6AA, United Kingdom for a brochure (tel. +44 (0)1908 858793; fax +44 (0)1908 858787; email ouw-customer-services@open.ac.uk).

The Open University
Walton Hall, Milton Keynes
MK7 6AA

First published 2011.

Edited and designed by The Open University.

Typeset by SR Nova Pvt. Ltd, Bangalore, India.

Printed in the United Kingdom by Latimer Trend and Company Ltd, Plymouth.

ISBN 978 1 8487 3347 3

1.1

Contents

Part 1 The information society

You can find this part of the block online. A link is provided on the TU100 website.

Part 2 Who owns 'me'?

You can find this part of the block online. A link is provided on the TU100 website.

Part 3 Keeping secrets

Part 4 Digital rights, digital wrongs

Part 1

The information society

Author: David Chapman

You can find this part of the block online. A link is provided on the TU100 website.

Part 2

Who owns 'me'?

Author: Linda Robson

You can find this part of the block online. A link is provided on the TU100 website.

Part 3

Keeping secrets

Author: Neil Smith

Introduction

This part of TU100 is about privacy and information security. It's about how to keep information secret when you want it to be, and how to keep it safe and unaltered even when you want it public. To start you thinking about some of the issues involved, read the short case study in Box 1.

Box 1 Child benefit data goes missing

In October 2007, the National Audit Office (NAO) asked HM Revenue and Customs (HMRC) for details of all child benefit claimants in the UK. They wanted the data to check a sample of claims and payments, to ensure that HMRC was paying child benefit correctly. The NAO only wanted the names, national insurance numbers and child benefit numbers of the claimants. However, HMRC decided that extracting just this data was too expensive, so they downloaded the entire child benefit database onto two CD-ROMs. This download included all the data the NAO wanted, and also the addresses, birth dates and bank details of everyone on the database, parents and children alike. The data identified 7.25 million adults and 15.5 million children. The discs were put in the internal post to the NAO.

They never arrived.

No one knows what happened to the discs, but the scope for identity theft and fraud was enormous. Name, address and date of birth are often sufficient to open a bank account in someone's name, or gain access to an existing one. Knowing details of new child benefit claimants could help abusive partners to terrorise their exes. I'm sure you can come up with many more ways in which the data could be misused, especially now you've worked through the previous part of this block.

The fact that none of this came to pass is probably down to luck.

You've already considered the social and personal aspects of information security in the previous two parts. You've looked at what information others have about you, what information you have about others, and what information you have and want to keep to yourself. You also know why information security is important. This part focuses on the technical aspects of information security and how to put it in place and maintain it. In the case of the child benefit example (Box 1), the techniques you learn about here would have secured the data on those CD-ROMs so that no one would have cared that they'd gone missing: the data would be inaccessible to anyone but the intended recipient.

The first session of this part looks at information security, what it is, and what can go wrong. Sessions 2 and 3 form a tour of cryptography, one very powerful technique that addresses many security concerns. Session 4 is a 'handbook' of the steps you should be taking to keep your information secure, and should be read as a continuation of the advice given in the previous part.

Learning outcomes

Your study of this part will help you to do the following.

Knowledge and understanding

- Describe the basic principles of information security and show how they apply to a range of situations.
- Describe, and explain the differences between, steganography, codes and ciphers.
- Describe, and explain the difference between, substitution and transposition in ciphers.
- Describe, and explain the difference between, monoalphabetic and polyalphabetic ciphers.
- Describe, and explain the difference between, symmetric and asymmetric ciphers.
- Outline the strengths and weaknesses of a variety of ciphers.
- Describe the concept of digital signatures and digital certificates, and how they can be used to provide assurance of authenticity and non-repudiation.
- Understand the notion of a one-way function and how ciphers can be based on such functions.

Cognitive skills

- Use a variety of ciphers to encipher and decipher information.
- Use a variety of techniques to break simple ciphers.

Key skills

- Identify and analyse a range of documents that are relevant to a topic.
- Evaluate the relevance and value of a document in relation to a research task.
- Synthesise a variety of sources into a coherent view of a topic.

Practical and professional skills

- Perform a basic information security audit.
- Identify the vulnerabilities of, and threats to, a range of information assets.
- Propose and implement simple actions to increase information security for individuals or small teams.
- Use Sense to apply complex functions (such as encryption and decryption functions) to data represented as text and numbers.
- Use Sense to process large data sets stored as files.

1 Information security

In this session you will look at what it means for information to be secure and what the threats are to that security. As part of this you will conduct a short research activity, putting into use some of the skills you've been developing throughout TU100.

1.1 Information security principles

The guiding principles behind information security are summed up in the acronym *CIA*, standing for *confidentiality*, *integrity* and *accessibility*. We want our information to be read by only the right people (confidentiality), we want it to stay the same all the time we're not changing it (integrity), and we want to be able to read and use the information whenever we want (accessibility). It is important to be able to distinguish between these three aspects of security.

In the child benefit example (Box 1), for instance, confidentiality was violated: there was a chance that unauthorised people could read the data. However, authorised users still had full access to the data, so it remained accessible; and the data was not changed, so its integrity was preserved.

As another example, in October 2009, Microsoft announced that it had lost all the server-held data for its line of Sidekick phones. As users were encouraged to store all their data (including contact details and photos) on servers, that meant that most users lost everything. In this case accessibility was violated, though there was no loss of confidentiality (no unauthorised persons got hold of users' data) nor was the data's integrity violated.

Activity 1 (self-assessment)

In this activity you are asked to consider two examples relating to information security. For each example, briefly describe which of the CIA principles were violated and why.

(a) The death of Ma.gnolia

By 2006, social bookmarking had emerged as a big thing in the Web 2.0 world (recall that bookmarking involves people sharing web resources that they like with their friends and other communities). In 2006, a new social bookmarking site called Ma.gnolia was launched. It used open standards and made its data easily available to other programs, services and websites. This was attractive to early

adopters, who tend to form the active core of a community that then attracts more users. Ma.gnolia quickly grew and was on a trajectory to become a significant player in social bookmarking. Things were looking promising.

On 30 January 2009, the site went down. For some reason, the database storing all the user-contributed data had become corrupt and all the data was lost. Even worse, the backups of the database were also corrupted. Ma.gnolia lost all details of its users and their bookmarks.

By the time the site relaunched in September 2009, the damage was done. With no archived data available, Ma.gnolia relaunched with a virtually empty set of social bookmarks and users. The early adopters who had created the initial bookmarks (and hence given the site its initial value) had moved on to the new site du jour. Ma.gnolia never reacquired a critical mass of users. It limped on for another year, but closed its doors permanently in November 2010.

(b) Twitter vs the Iranian Cyber Army

On 18 December 2009, a group of hackers calling themselves the Iranian Cyber Army took over the website of Twitter. Visitors to the Twitter.com site were presented with a page announcing 'THIS SITE HAS BEEN HACKED BY IRANIAN CYBER ARMY' and containing a message protesting against the actions of the USA.

The hackers hadn't touched Twitter's own servers. Instead, they attacked the domain name system (DNS), the service that converts textual hostnames (such as twitter.com) into the IP addresses that computers use to find each other (such as 128.242.245.20). The effect of the attack was that a request to access the Twitter website returned a site run by the hackers. However, other ways of accessing Twitter information (such as using third-party clients) were unaffected.

Twitter was down for an hour or two, and the Iranian Cyber Army have since attacked a number of other sites.

When we consider communication, we also need two additional principles: *authentication* and *non-repudiation*. When we receive a message, we want to be confident that it really came from the person we think it came from (authentication); we also don't want the sender to turn round later and say they didn't really send it (non-repudiation), especially if we've gone to some expense acting on their original message.

Digital signatures were mentioned in Part 1 as a way of ensuring authentication and non-repudiation. I describe how they work in Session 4 below.

Activity 2 (exploratory)

When you receive an email purporting to come from your mum (say), how do you know that it really came from her? The fact that the headers say 'From: Your Mum' will probably give you a clue – but should you rely on that?

Most email clients allow you to create additional identities. The details will vary depending on the email client you use. Your client's help files should tell you how to do it, and instructions for some popular mail clients are in the 'Email clients' wiki on the resources page associated with this part.

If the instructions for your email client aren't in the wiki, please add them.

Alter your email account settings to change the sender identity. Send some messages (to people you know) with this new identity, and ask them to do the same for you. Now how much do you trust that that message really was from your mum?

The different requirements for information security are not always as they first appear. Consider, for a moment, the security needs for transmitting an order to launch nuclear missiles. I imagine your first thought would be that the order needs to be encrypted so that it remains confidential. Yet confidentiality isn't the first requirement. Most of the time, both sides in a conflict will be aware that it's moving to nuclear brinkmanship, so the mere presence of such an order won't be much of a shock. It also doesn't much matter if the enemy can quickly read the contents of the order (for example, to discover the target). They'll find out soon enough when the missiles are launched, and there's probably not much they can do about it anyway. An extra few minutes are unlikely to make a great deal of difference, so there's not much lost by sending the order 'in the clear' (i.e. unencrypted). However, what that order does need is authentication. The recipient of the order will need to be very, very sure that it is a genuine order from someone who really does have the authority to give it.

1.2 Information assets

To start this section, I want you to consider how you might ideally maximise the security of valuable information.

Activity 3 (exploratory)

Suppose you need to store some information – let's say a hundred words or so, not necessarily in an electronic format.

(a) How could you store it so that it was as confidential as possible?

(b) How could you store it so that it was as unchangeable as possible?

(c) How could you store it so that it was as accessible to you as possible?

Would you call any of these approaches 'useful'?

Comment

(a) The best approach to confidentiality is summed up in a Russian proverb: 'It's easy for two people to keep a secret. So long as one of them is dead.' If I really wanted to keep some information secret, I'd destroy every physical copy of it that exists. If I was really paranoid, I'd have to kill everyone else who knew the secret. This approach is of limited practical application, but is a staple of a certain kind of spy fiction.

(b) If I want information to not change over time (i.e. to maintain its integrity), the best technology I've got available to me is to write it into wet clay, bake it and bury it. The Mesopotamians did that about six thousand years ago and we can still read what they wrote.

(c) If I want maximum accessibility then tattooing the information in glow-in-the-dark ink on my forearm would be a good start.

None of these approaches are all that useful. Killing all your friends is likely to make you unpopular, baked clay tablets aren't that portable, and tattooing isn't the best option for handling changing data, or even large volumes. (Though I have just read a news article on cheating in exams in which a student had written the answers on his forearm, blended in with all the tattoos already there.)

As you discovered in the previous activity, security isn't an absolute thing. You have to balance how much security you want for your valuable information – your *information assets* – against the drawbacks of that security. One way to do this is to examine the ways your information could be at risk, how likely each of these risks is to come to pass, and how much damage such security breaches would cause. Only then can you determine what a proportionate response would be to prevent those breaches.

The damage done by a security breach could also vary in different situations (see Box 2 for one real-world example). The potential cost of someone getting access to your bank account is easy to quantify. But how much effort should you go to in order to secure sentimental information? For instance, all my photos of my children are kept digitally. If I lost all my digital information in a fire or a catastrophic disk failure, I would lose all those photos. The financial loss would be trivial, but the emotional loss would be huge.

Box 2 Stuxnet

Information security isn't just constrained to the ethereal world of information. Failures in information security can have significant effects in the real world. Most large industrial plants, such as oil refineries, chemical plants, nuclear power stations and the like, are controlled by networks of computerised supervisory control and data acquisition (SCADA) controllers. While most of these networks aren't connected to the internet, they do have Windows PCs that act as controllers and terminals for staff. Those PCs, and the specific software for driving the machinery, are vulnerable to malware coming in on USB memory sticks. That's been a theoretical vulnerability – until now.

At the time of writing (late 2010), the information security community is alive with speculation about a piece of malware called Stuxnet. This is a very complex piece of software that is infecting PCs across the world. It announces its legitimacy to the host computer with digital signatures from two Taiwanese chip manufacturers. It was first noted in June 2010 by VirusBlokA, a Belarusian security firm, but had probably been circulating in the wild since 2009.

Stuxnet is notable for two reasons. First, it specifically targets industrial controllers. Indeed, given some of the details of the Stuxnet program code, it seems to be targeting one specific industrial site. It's spreading itself across many PCs not to cause damage there but to allow itself to spread to the target site, one infection at a time. Second, it's a large and complex piece of software that uses at least four different methods to get itself onto uninfected computers. Stuxnet isn't the sort of thing that a few teenagers could quickly knock up in their bedroom on a wet afternoon; its creation must have required the sorts of resources that only large entities, such as national governments, can bring to bear.

At the time of going to press, no one has owned up to creating Stuxnet or to having been damaged by it, but the countries most affected by it are Iran, Pakistan, India and Indonesia. It targets a particular type of high-speed motor controller that is manufactured in Iran and Finland. The export of similar types of motor controller from the USA is restricted by the US government, as such controllers can be used to run the centrifuges that refine uranium for use in nuclear power stations and nuclear weapons. It appears that Iran has recently had problems with its nuclear refinement centrifuges, caused by computer issues. The recent assassinations of several Iranian nuclear scientists, including Iran's

Recall from Block 1 Part 1 that malware is malicious software designed to enter computer systems without the knowledge of the owner. You will find out more about it shortly.

top expert on Stuxnet, could just be coincidence. Is Stuxnet a US–Israeli cyber-weapon aimed at the Iranian nuclear programme? We'll probably never know. But the damage caused to the Iranian nuclear programme is at least as great as would result from an airstrike, without the political backlash that comes from flying cruise missiles into other countries.

Before you can take steps to protect your valuable information, you need to know what information you have that needs protection: your valuable information assets. Therefore in the next activity, you'll identify the information you want to protect. I will then pick this up in the following section by considering what kinds of risks there can be to different kinds of information, as well as some ways to protect information from those risks.

Activity 4 (exploratory)

Catalogue five of your information assets that need protection. What would be the costs (financial, emotional, personal, etc.) of that information being rendered inaccessible, non-confidential, or changed without your authorisation? Lay out your answer in the form of a table, with the CIA criteria as columns and the information assets as rows. Table 1 shows an example in which I have considered my digital photos. Remember that information doesn't just reside in a computer – also consider information on paper, as printed photographs, etc.

Table 1 Information assets and costs: example

Asset	Cost of confidentiality breach	Cost of integrity breach	Cost of accessibility breach
Digital photos	Exposure could cause embarrassment or unwanted attention. I've also taken photos of high-value items at home, to justify insurance claims should they be necessary. That could make me a target for thieves.	Changed photos are likely to be corrupt, perhaps losing some of the image. Changed metadata (such as when and where taken) could cause a lot of confusion.	The sentimental loss could be large. It could also make insurance claims more difficult.

Comment
Your catalogue may contain some of the items shown in Table 2.

Table 2 Information assets and costs

Asset	Cost of confidentiality breach	Cost of integrity breach	Cost of accessibility breach
TU100 notes and TMA submissions	Not a big issue for me, but could make plagiarism easier for others.	Could be a major problem, as I might have to put a lot of effort into checking and recreating them.	Very similar to integrity: I'd have to recreate them, if they're not on a backup.
My email accounts at home and work	Could contain confidential or sensitive information I'd rather not share. That could cause financial loss, embarrassment, or unwanted attention if I hold unpopular views.	If someone has access to my email account, they could send messages that purport to be from me. The consequences could range from a bit of a giggle to committing me to significant financial outlay.	I keep a lot of details about what I should be doing each day in my email accounts. If I lost those, I'd lose much of my agenda.
Bought music and book downloads	Some embarrassment possible over my playlists. Potential for large lawsuits if my files end up on file-sharing sites and can be traced back to me.	A changed (corrupt) music file probably won't play. A changed book may be unintelligible or, perhaps worse, misleading.	Either the cost of re-buying the items, or the time taken to persuade the supplier that I'm entitled to another download.
Financial records, mostly paper	The potential for embarrassment and awkward moments with friends and family could be huge. Much of the information could be used as the basis for identity theft and fraud.	If someone changes the content of my bank account without my knowing then the potential costs are huge, both directly and in respect of the damage to my credit rating.	Some time and perhaps cost incurred requesting copies of the documents.
Mobile phone	Can access email and various secure websites, so an unauthorised person getting hold of the phone would result in all those accounts being compromised, plus details of my family, friends and colleagues.	Nothing on my phone is the definitive copy of anything (apart from a few casual photos), so corruption of data won't be a problem if I'm aware of it.	Not having a phone would force me to make some changes to my routine, but nothing too significant until I can get a replacement or repair.

Your list will include other items, I'm sure.

For many items, the costs of security breaches are very similar in kind, if not in degree. For instance, the consequences of losing a licence for DRM-controlled songs are similar to those of losing a licence for some software I've bought.

1.3 Vulnerabilities and threats

Now you know what information assets you have, it's time to look at how those assets can be compromised. A *vulnerability* is a point at which there is potential for a security breach. A *threat* is some danger that can exploit a vulnerability. A *countermeasure* is something you do to protect your information against threats and vulnerabilities.

In this section you will learn about some different kinds of threat, the vulnerabilities that they exploit and some countermeasures that can be put in place to guard against them. Rather than me telling you all about the different threats, you will carry out some research to find out about them. Throughout this module you've been learning how to find, assess and read documents from a variety of sources. This section will first show you how to summarise and synthesise information from a number of sources. You will then put that into practice in researching some major information security threats. Session 2 will go into more detail about countermeasures.

Research techniques

First, let's look at some techniques that you can use for doing your research. You will be doing three things:

1 making notes about and summarising things you read

2 combining notes from different sources

3 identifying gaps in knowledge and finding ways to plug them.

This process is repeated until you have done enough to fulfil your purpose.

The first task, making notes and summarising what you have read, is something you've been doing a lot throughout your study.

The next two tasks (combining notes and finding gaps) are probably less familiar, so I'll spend a few minutes now showing you how to perform them.

Activity 5 (exploratory)

When researching an area of knowledge, it is always a good idea to collect your information from more than one source. Write down three advantages of using more than one source when investigating a particular subject.

Comment

Using more than one source allows you to:

- Verify information you already have. Although you have previously looked at using the PROMPT criteria for judging the reliability of sources, being able to find material elsewhere that confirms what a source says further strengthens its trustworthiness.

- Provide a more rounded picture of the subject matter. Each source provides information from its own particular perspective. Furthermore, no source on its own can include everything.

- Allow you to pick and choose the information that you think is relevant to your own particular purposes. Remember that other writers may well have had different objectives from you when compiling their information.

You may have thought of others.

Now consider the two web articles below, both of which describe spam. The first is from Wikipedia, while the second is from the About.com website. Read them both and then answer the questions in the activity that follows.

> Spam is the use of electronic messaging systems (including most broadcast media, digital delivery systems) to send unsolicited bulk messages indiscriminately. While the most widely recognized form of spam is e-mail spam, the term is applied to similar abuses in other media: instant messaging spam, Usenet newsgroup spam, Web search engine spam, spam in blogs, wiki spam, online classified ads spam, mobile phone messaging spam, Internet forum spam, junk fax transmissions, social networking spam, television advertising and file sharing network spam.
>
> Spamming remains economically viable because advertisers have no operating costs beyond the management of their mailing lists, and it is difficult to hold senders accountable for their mass mailings. Because the barrier to entry is so low, spammers are numerous, and the volume of unsolicited mail has become very high. [...] The costs, such as lost productivity and fraud, are borne by the public and by Internet service providers, which have been forced to add extra capacity to cope with the deluge. Spamming has been the subject of legislation in many jurisdictions.
>
> People who create electronic spam are called *spammers*.
>
> Wikipedia, 2011

Spam: either you have already encountered it or you do not use email. If the latter is the case, spam is a good reason not starting using email; it is probably also the only reason.

What Spam Is

An exact definition of "spam", should it exist would probably not be agreed upon by many. This is because and why any definition of junk email includes a subjective part – "I recognize a spam when I see it!".

- Emails you did not ask for that were
- sent in bulk
- from senders you do not know

are suspicious of being spam.

Newsletters you did sign up for, an email from a college friend and messages from people trying to contact you personally are, of course, not spam. A newsletter somebody signed you up for to annoy you is not spam but a different kind of email abuse. An email sent to you in bulk by an unknown sender that you do in fact welcome and find useful may not be spam either.

Every email you asked for is not spam but not every email you did not ask for is spam. For practical means, there is no point in sophistic examination of all the reasons that can, could or must not justify the junk status of any email (if you enjoy the sophistic exercise, do go ahead!).

I used to include an example of a junk email message in this space but I'll point to your *Inbox* or, if you are graced with a potent spam filter, *Spam* folder instead.

Why Spam Is

The reason spam is thriving is none other than it works (for it to be a pyramid scheme spam has been around for too long). People do buy products advertised in junk email. Don't (if you do not like spam, of course).

Spam works because it is so cheap to send. Using means ranging from spam-friendly ISPs to ordinary people's computers turned spam-machines, spammers can send their junk inexpensively. At the same time, the risk of getting caught is substantial and involves dear costs – apparently not enough to offset the profitability of sending spam.

Why Spam is Bad

Spam is bad because the cost is borne by the recipient. Spam costs time, money and resources, making email a significantly less attractive medium. Fortunately, spam has not ruined it completely, though, and neither will it.

Tschabitscher, 2011 (About.com)

Activity 6 (exploratory)

(a) What key points are shared by the two articles?

(b) What things are different?

(c) Suppose you were researching material for a report on how individual users can protect themselves from spam.

    (i)   How might the shared points or differences that you noted in parts (a) and (b) prompt you to continue your research?

    (ii) Is there anything in the articles that you think is irrelevant to that purpose?

Comment

(a) The two articles have important overlaps: they define the term 'spam' in broadly similar ways and they discuss the places where spam can be found. Both mention the economic conditions that allow spammers to flourish as well as the difficulties in prosecuting them. The fact that two different articles agree on these points, without one being an obvious copy of the other, suggests that there is some merit in these points.

(b) The Wikipedia article discusses different forms of spam other than email – for example, it counts television advertising as a form of spam. The About.com article defines the term 'spam' more narrowly, referring only to email.

(c) (i) The About.com article mentions that spam can be sent by home PCs that have been turned into 'spam machines'. This looks like a promising avenue for future research.

    (ii) Both articles discuss the economics of spam and the futility of passing laws to block it. Whilst this is good to know, it is unlikely to be anything that an individual can influence to reduce how much spam they receive.

Spray diagrams are a pictorial way of showing the main concepts in a subject area and how they're connected. You've met them before in this module. To create a spray diagram, start with the key topic that the diagram will be about and draw lines from it leading to each related concept. If that concept has sub-ideas, make more lines.

It's easier to see what I mean with an example. Figure 1 shows the spray diagram that I created from the Wikipedia article on spam. You should be able to see that it captures the main points of the article. Also note that I connected some of the concepts with arrows that go across the diagram: that's to show that these ideas are connected, even when they appear in different sections of the diagram.

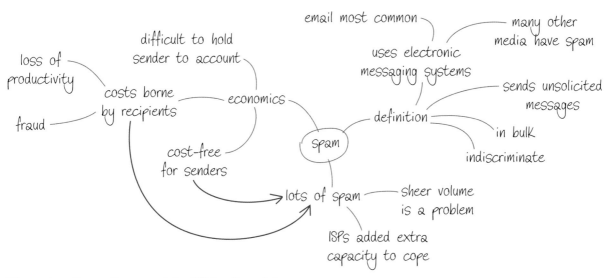

Figure 1   Spray diagram of the Wikipedia article on spam

Activity 7 (exploratory)

Draw your own spray diagram from the second (About.com) article on spam.

Comment

Figure 2 shows my diagram. Yours will of course be different, but I hope it mentions similar things and has a somewhat similar structure.

If you use spray diagrams to represent your ideas, you should bear two things in mind. First, they're good for representing the high-level concepts in a subject area; if you want to keep track of details, writing traditional notes is often easier. Second, you can draw your spray diagrams however you want to, but as your understanding of the area develops you'll find yourself revising and restructuring your early diagrams. This is easier if you use a tool such as FreeMind to draw your spray diagrams, rather than doing them on paper.

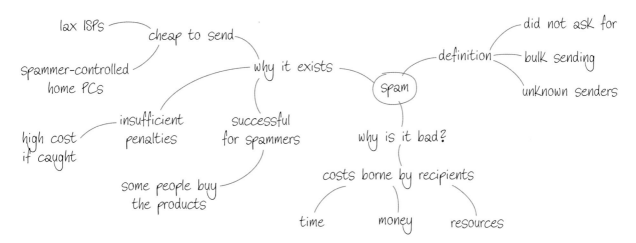

Figure 2   Spray diagram of the About.com article on spam

Activity 8 (exploratory)

Now that you have taken notes from different sources on the same subject, you will need to combine them into a coherent whole. Try forming a single spray diagram that represents the main ideas from both the Wikipedia and the About.com articles.

Comment

Figure 3 shows my diagram.

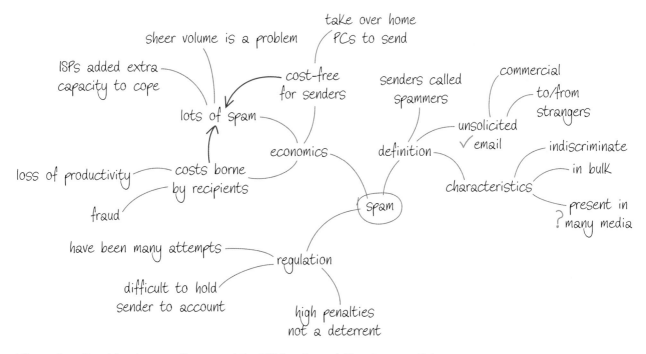

Figure 3   Combined spray diagram of the Wikipedia and About.com articles

Again, yours will be different. You'll notice that it's not just a merging of the two diagrams: branches of each diagram have been rearranged and merged. You'll also notice that I've annotated two of the notes on the definition of spam. This is because the two articles agreed that unsolicited email is spam, but disagreed on what else could be considered spam.

The last skill you need to have in order to research a subject area is the ability to determine what questions to ask. Reading random articles is unlikely to get you very far with understanding a new topic. You might think to consult a resource such as Wikipedia, which is a fair starting point – but it is no more than that, as Box 3 explains. If you're searching online for articles, you need to know what search terms to use to start with. The more methodical you are about this, the more straightforward the process. Where a document mentions a topic or phrase that you don't know about, but the author in question seems to think it is important, make a note of it and follow up any references made to that topic. For instance, the About.com article above talked about spam, but also mentioned taking over home PCs. You may not know much about this, but it sounds as though it could be relevant to understanding information security threats. If someone can take over your PC to send spam, what else could they do with it?

Box 3 Academic use of Wikipedia

Wikipedia is a controversial source of information in academic circles. By all means use it in your studies, but it is important to understand its limitations and thus use it wisely.

Wikipedia is an excellent source of overviews on subjects, but its wiki nature means that what you read there could be the result of some prankster changing the article to include content that is untrue or just misinformed. This means that information you find on Wikipedia is inherently unreliable and hence suspect. You shouldn't trust anything you read on Wikipedia: it all needs to be verified against more reliable sources.

However, the majority of Wikipedia articles are mostly accurate and are often very good summaries of the topic in question. When I need to find out about something, Wikipedia is often my first port of call. It gives me an overview of the topic, suggests which questions I should ask, and provides some pointers to more reliable sources. So Wikipedia may be where I start my research, but it is certainly not where I finish.

When you come across new topics and areas like this, make a note of them and, when you've finished the article you're reading, spend a few minutes looking up definitions and so on. If the new topic seems relevant, add it to your list of things to investigate further. If it isn't, just make a note of it and move on.

Researching threats

You're now in a position to investigate some of the more significant information security threats. The next activity will guide you through this. Note that in this activity you'll be doing two things. First, you'll be learning about information security threats, which are something that it's useful for ICT experts to know about. Second, you'll be practising your research skills, which you'll find useful in subsequent studies and more widely.

Activity 9 (exploratory)

The main threats you should consider, as a private individual or in the context of a small organisation, are the following:

(a) threats to your PC and other devices that arise from malicious software (viruses, worms and the like, collectively termed *malware*)

Types of malware include *spyware* and *adware*.

(b) threats to your communications (such as *spam* and *denial of service (DoS)* or *distributed denial of service (DDoS) attacks*, often launched by *botnets*)

(c) threats that target your human judgement (such as *phishing* and other scams).

For each of these topics, research and make notes on what the threats are, how they originate, how they can be recognised, and some examples of damage or loss caused when such threats materialise. Also note which of the CIA principles are violated by these threats. You will notice that some key words are italicised: you should make notes on their meanings as part of your research.

You should try to draw on the kinds of resources and services that you have been guided to use in TU100 so far – the Library, advanced Google searching, technology news websites and magazines, and so on.

You can record your notes in any way you like, but you need to ensure that there is sufficient detail for you to understand the notes when you return to them later. Spray diagrams are good for showing the key concepts and how they are connected; text notes are good for recording detail. You may want to share your notes with your tutor group, perhaps on a shared wiki page.

Finally, this activity can be a terrible time sink. Don't spend more than an hour reading and making notes, and don't get sucked into chasing down details of one particular threat – make sure you end up with an overview of all the threats I mentioned above. There's no need for you to transform your notes and/or spray diagrams into an essay or report.

Comment

I created the spray diagram shown in Figure 4. Your notes may cover some different subjects, but they should include descriptions of the key terms from the question.

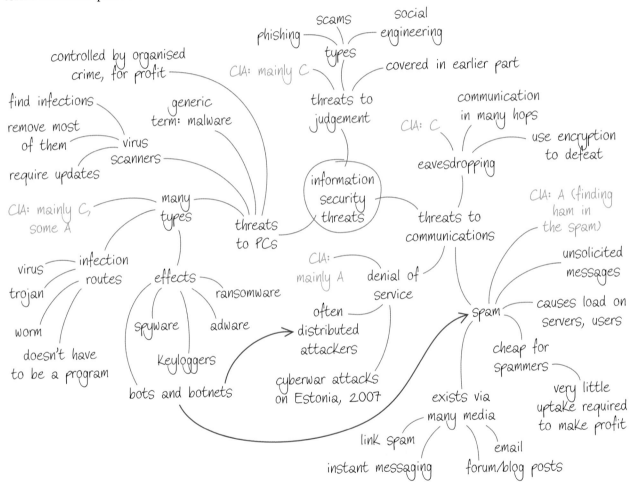

Figure 4   **Spray diagram of information security threats**

1.4 Conclusion

In this session I introduced you to some key principles of information security. You catalogued your valuable information as assets that need securing. Finally, you researched some security threats, finding out about the damage that can be done and what can be done to protect against specific kinds of threat.

This session should have helped you with the following learning outcomes.

- Describe the basic principles of information security and show how they apply to a range of situations.
- Identify and analyse a range of documents that are relevant to a topic.
- Evaluate the relevance and value of a document in relation to a research task.
- Synthesise a variety of sources into a coherent view of a topic.
- Perform a basic information security audit.
- Identify the vulnerabilities of, and threats to, a range of information assets.

Cryptography

2

In the last session, you examined how information security can be easily compromised. In that session you largely concentrated on information held in one place, but the problems increase with information on the move. How can information that is being sent from person to person be protected? Recall that the internet is a packet-switched network where messages pass across many machines as they traverse the network, so the opportunities for eavesdropping are rife.

In this session you will explore how cryptography answers these sorts of questions. Alongside learning about the underlying concepts, in order to gain an appreciation of the impact of the advent of computers on cryptography you will carry out several practical activities using Sense. This session is therefore likely to require more study time than the other sessions in this part.

2.1 The role of cryptography

The answer to protecting information on the move lies with disguising the message to prevent anyone from reading it unless they know the trick. You learned in Block 1 Part 6 that one way to do this is to encode it using an algorithm and a *key*. For instance, you could use the code wheel shown in Figure 5 to encode a message. The inner wheel can turn to any position against the outer wheel. The algorithm is 'to encode a

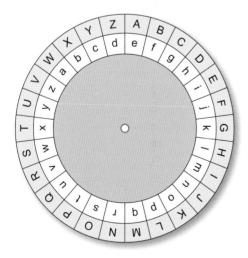

Figure 5   A code wheel

letter, find it on the inner wheel and replace it with the corresponding letter on the outer wheel'. To decode an encoded message this algorithm can simply be applied in reverse. The key is the letter on the outer wheel that corresponds to 'a' on the inner wheel (W in the case of the figure): this specifies the alignment of the outer wheel against the inner wheel. If others don't know both the algorithm and the key, any message you encode is protected – until, of course, someone breaks your code. The key for the code is typically much smaller than the information we want to protect, so it's easier to secure the key than the original message.

Cryptography is the science of codes and ciphers, and it is widely used – though it's rarely recognised. It's cryptography that makes secure websites (those using the HTTPS protocol) secure. If you're setting up an email program and have to make choices about IMAPS, TLS and SSL, all those Ss mean 'secure' and that's cryptography again. When you set up a wireless network at home and use WPA2 protection, this works to secure all traffic on your network. Virtual private networks (VPNs) do a similar thing: all traffic between your computer and the host network is sent through an encrypted 'tunnel'. It's also the basis of digital rights management (DRM), the technology that ensures only authorised users can access copyrighted content (you'll find out more about DRM in the next part). Cryptography also plays a crucial role in national security (see Box 4). The list goes on!

> You may recall that WPA2 is the recommended security protocol for Wi-Fi networks.

Box 4 Governments and cryptography

The relationship between governments and cryptography is best described as 'it's complicated'. On the one hand, governments support large cryptographic organisations such as the UK's GCHQ and the USA's NSA. Governments need these institutions, both to ensure their own communications remain secret and to break the cryptography of other states. Yet at the same time, states are wary of allowing secure cryptographic techniques to get into the hands of private individuals. They don't want criminals to be able to communicate with each other with no possibility of law enforcement agencies being able to eavesdrop on them. To offset this danger, the Regulation of Investigatory Powers Act (RIPA) in UK law requires you to hand over your encryption keys when demanded by the authorities.

The USA classes some cryptographic techniques as munitions and prevents their export, much as it prevents the export of bombs. In 1993, Phil Zimmermann was the subject of criminal investigations by the US government for writing and distributing the home-use encryption package PGP (Pretty Good Privacy). The case collapsed soon after Zimmermann published the source code of PGP as a book, which has no export restrictions.

In 2010, the government of the United Arab Emirates threatened to ban Blackberry devices. This was because the Blackberry, a brand of smart phone made by RIM, stores the user's emails on secure servers, with the email traffic between the server and the device being strongly encrypted. The UAE government didn't like not being able to eavesdrop on emails sent and received in the country. Eventually a (secret) settlement was reached, which probably involves RIM allowing the UAE government access to UAE subscribers' emails if instructed to do so by a court order.

2.2 Steganography, codes and ciphers

Most of cryptography is concerned with keeping information secret during communication, as that's a harder problem than keeping secrets in one place. To make discussions easier, cryptographers use a standard cast of characters to describe what's going on.

Hello, Alice and Bob

The two stars of the cryptography show are *Alice* and *Bob*. Alice wants to send a message to Bob, and wants to ensure that no one does anything unpleasant to it on the way. Unfortunately, *Eve* the eavesdropper is listening in on the conversation: she can read everything that Alice and Bob send to each other. In addition *Mallory*, the malicious attacker, is both reading and altering the messages in transit. Figure 6 shows the situation.

There is a whole host of other standard characters used in the cryptography literature, but I'll restrict myself to just Alice, Bob, Eve and Mallory.

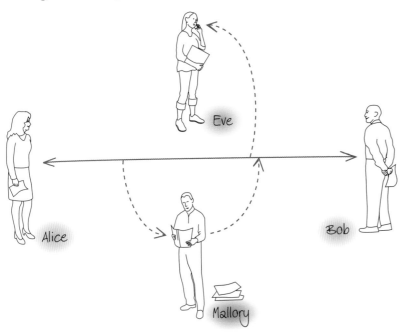

Figure 6   Alice, Bob, Eve and Mallory

Alice and Bob need to be assured that the content of their messages is not being read by Eve (confidentiality) and that any changes made by Mallory are detected (integrity).

There are three ways to keep messages away from prying eyes, which I will discuss in this section: steganography, codes and ciphers.

Steganography

Steganography is the art of hiding a message so that potential eavesdroppers don't even know it is there. This is all the James Bond stuff of hidden compartments and invisible ink.

Much early message passing relied on steganography, simply hiding the message so that enemies couldn't see it. The first known mention of secret writing occurs in *The Histories*, written by Herodotus around 440 BCE. He lived during the conflict between the expanding Greek world and the declining Persian Empire, and descriptions of these battles became part of *The Histories*. In Book Seven, Herodotus tells of Demaratus, a Greek exile in the Persian Empire who had become a confidant of the Persian Emperor Xerxes the Great. Persian plans to invade Greece had come to Demaratus' attention; despite being out of favour in his native country, he was sufficiently concerned to send word to the Greeks.

> As soon as news reached [Demaratus] at Susa that Xerxes had decided upon the invasion of Greece, he felt that he must pass on the information to Sparta. As the danger of discovery was great, there was only one way in which he could contrive to get the message through: this was by scraping the wax off a pair of wooden folding tablets, writing on the wood underneath what Xerxes intended to do, and then covering the message over with wax again. In this way the tablets, being apparently blank, would cause no trouble with the guards along the road. When the message reached its destination, no one was able to guess the secret until, as I understand, Cleomenes' daughter Gorgo, who was the wife of Leonidas, divined it and told the others that, if they scraped the wax off, they would find something written on the wood underneath. This was done; the message was revealed and read, and afterwards passed on to the other Greeks. That, at any rate, is the story of what happened.

Herodotus, *The Histories*, Book Seven, Section 239

Steganography is still alive and well in the twenty-first century. In the middle of 2010, a ring of Russian spies was exposed by the US authorities. They had been passing messages back to their handlers by hiding them in image files, which were then posted to publicly accessible websites.

This technique works because each pixel in a coloured image is represented by three numbers, specifying the amount of red, green and blue at that point. Typically, images use one byte to represent each colour at each pixel. Since one byte can represent $2^8 = 256$ variations on that one colour, there are $256^3 = 16\,777\,216$ possible combinations of the three colours. This is more than the human eye can distinguish: a small change in the colour values of a pixel has no noticeable effect. Thus you can use, say, the least significant bit of each byte to store hidden information.

For instance, if the first six bytes of an image file are

    11100010 11110000 10001110
    01001000 10101011 10001001

and we want to encode the number 22 (binary form 010110), we can change the last bits of these six bytes to represent that number:

    1110001**0** 1111000**1** 1000111**0**
    0100100**1** 1010101**1** 1000100**0**

If we now read the file and look at the least significant bits, we can recover the hidden message (the number 22).

As the values of these bits are pretty much random anyway, the hidden information is unlikely to be detected. Indeed, the Russian spies' communications went entirely unnoticed by the US authorities until they became aware of the spies through other means.

Codes

In cryptography circles, a *code* is a way of representing large chunks of messages by single signals. For instance, the code phrase 'The swallows have flown east' may mean 'The entire operation has been blown! Run for your life!' Another example is the flag messages that Napoleonic navies used to communicate between ships. The advantage of a code is that eavesdroppers may not even realise that a message has been passed. Even if they do, they have no way of cracking the code from intercepting messages alone. The disadvantage is that the code has a built-in limit on the messages it can convey.

Codes and codes

'Code' is an overloaded word in computing circles. In cryptography, a code is something that represents words or phrases.

More generally, a 'code' is used to name how information is represented in a different medium. For instance, Morse code is a way of representing letters as the dots and dashes that can be sent over telegraph cables, and Unicode is a way of representing the

same letters with numbers that computers can understand. These types of code aren't intended to conceal anything.

Pushing the idea further, 'codes' are often used to robustly represent numerically represented information in the presence of transmission or storage errors. The code defines which digit is used and how it is calculated. (The added digit is termed a check digit.) For instance, the last digit of a credit card number is used to check that the previous digits have been entered correctly.

Finally, the term 'code' is often used by programmers to refer to programs, to the extent that many programmers refer to themselves as 'coders'.

Make sure that when you come across the word 'code', you know which meaning is intended.

Ciphers

Ciphers are used to encode small parts of messages separately, such as letter by letter. They have the advantage of great flexibility: any message can be transformed (*encrypted* or *enciphered*). The disadvantage is that analysing large chunks of encrypted text may allow an eavesdropper to work out the cipher and hence read the message.

Activity 10 (self-assessment)

In rugby line-outs each team needs to secretly arrange who the ball will be thrown to, so as to gain an advantage over their opponents. They do this by having the thrower shout predefined nonsense words to the team. (Quarterbacks in American football do the same thing with the calls they make to their team to describe the sort of play they will make.)

The team want to send hidden information. Is their method best described as steganography, a code or a cipher?

Another term for *cipher* is *encryption function*. A *decryption function* is used to decipher.

Ciphers work to transform the original message, termed *plaintext*, into an encrypted form termed the *ciphertext*. This transformation is controlled by the cipher algorithm (that is, the process it employs) and a key. To ensure that they can communicate safely, Alice and Bob need to agree both the algorithm and the key to be used. When Bob receives ciphertext from Alice, with the help of the key he uses his knowledge of the algorithm to *decrypt* (*decipher*) the ciphertext and recover the plaintext.

Activity 11 (exploratory)

All cryptographic systems require some form of key to tell the recipient how to decipher the message. How does this represent a weakness with cryptography?

Comment

The key needs to be secretly transmitted between Alice and Bob. If Eve can read the key as it's transmitted, she can read all subsequent communication using that key. This is called the key distribution problem, and is something I'll come back to in Section 4.2.

For a cipher to be a practical and safe method of communication, the key is typically much smaller than the information that needs to be protected, so it's easier to secure the key than the original data.

To help you understand how ciphers work, I'm going to have a look at some historical ciphers. I'm going to do this because many of the techniques used historically are still in use now, but they're easier to see in older and simpler ciphers. It also allows you to track the constant battle between codemakers and codebreakers – a battle that is still going on. And you'll be getting your hands dirty: several activities in this session use Sense to encipher and decipher text, as well as break some ciphers. Through this, as well as developing your programming skills you will begin to see the contribution made by computers to cryptography.

Despite the distinction between codes and ciphers, the term 'code' is often used generically. Codebreakers, for example, are more often than not involved in breaking ciphers.

2.3   Historic ciphers and the birth of computing

Ciphers have been used since about the time that people started writing messages. Many of them, unsurprisingly, were developed for intelligence or military applications. This remains true to this day.

Just like steganography, ciphers were used in the ancient world, and two of the most well-known ciphers nicely illustrate the two main kinds of cipher algorithm: *transposition* and *substitution*.

Transposition

Transposition simply means 'scrambling'. A cipher using this kind of algorithm rearranges the letters of a message, making it unintelligible to the uninitiated.

The *scytale* (rhymes with 'Italy') was a device that used transposition as a method of encryption. It was first described by Plutarch in the first century BCE. It consists of a wooden staff around which the sender wraps a strip of parchment. The sender writes the message on the wound strip (see Figure 7). When the strip is unwound, the letters are scrambled and

You can easily make your own scytale from a piece of paper, cut and taped into a long strip, and a broom handle. Hours (well, minutes) of fun.

the message can't be read. The recipient can decipher the message by wrapping the strip around an identical staff.

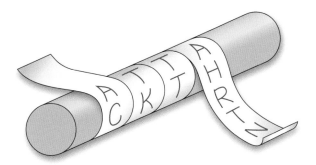

Figure 7   **A scytale in use**

Using a scytale is equivalent to filling in a grid. For example, if the scytale is thick enough to have five letters written around its circumference, that's equivalent to having a grid with five rows. The message is written in the grid, using just enough columns to fit the message into five rows. (To find the number of columns, divide the message length by the number of rows, rounding up.) Then the encrypted message is read by going down each column. For instance, the message

To keep things clear in this material, I'll use lower-case text for plaintext and UPPER-CASE TEXT for ciphertext.

attack the forts at dawn

will fill a five-row grid like this:

a	t	t	a
c	k	t	h
e	f	o	r
t	s	a	t
d	a	w	n

Notice I've taken out the spaces from the plaintext and ciphertext. This removes the clues for a codebreaker that come from looking at word lengths.

and the ciphertext can be read off by going down each column:

ACETDTKFSATTOAWAHRTN

For this kind of cipher, the key is the number of rows in the table (equivalently, the circumference of the staff).

Activity 12 (self-assessment)

Encipher the text attack the forts at dawn using a key of 3. (You'll need to work out how many columns to use.)

As you can see, the message is not easy to work out from the ciphertext alone, but decrypting it is as easy as filling in a table with the correct number of rows and columns and reading the message off.

Activity 13 (exploratory)

How would you go about decrypting a scytale-enciphered message if you didn't know the key?

Comment

Try each key in turn. First try a table with two rows and see if the decrypted message makes sense; then try a table with three rows; and so on until you get something intelligible.

Activity 14 (exploratory)

In this activity you will use Sense to encipher and decipher text using the scytale cipher. You will find the detailed instructions for it in the Sense activities section of the 'Study resources' page on the TU100 website.

Note that there are several Sense activities in this session, so if it is more convenient for you then you can wait until the end of the session before completing them as a set.

Substitution

Substitution involves replacing letters in the plaintext with letters, numbers or other symbols to make the ciphertext. The classic example of a substitution cipher is the *Caesar cipher*, as popularised by the self-effacing Julius Caesar. This cipher uses two alphabets, offset from each other (Figure 8). The plaintext is referred to in the top alphabet, while the ciphertext is the bottom alphabet. The key is the number of places that the ciphertext alphabet is offset; in Figure 8, the key is 3. This is essentially the cipher of Figure 5, albeit with a different key. Note that you can express the key as either the offset of the bottom alphabet or the letter in the bottom alphabet that is opposite the top 'a'.

a	b	c	d	e	f	g	h	i	j	k	l	m	n	o	p	q	r	s	t	u	v	w	x	y	z
D	E	F	G	H	I	J	K	L	M	N	O	P	Q	R	S	T	U	V	W	X	Y	Z	A	B	C

Figure 8   An example Caesar cipher

For a message to be enciphered, each letter in it is replaced with the corresponding letter from the bottom alphabet: a is encrypted as D, t as W, c as F and so on. So the plaintext attack the forts at dawn will be encrypted as DWWDFN WKH IRUWV DW GDZQ. To decipher a message, find each letter of the ciphertext in the bottom alphabet and replace it with the corresponding plaintext letter in the top alphabet.

Activity 15 (self-assessment)

(a) Encipher the message i like sausages using a Caesar cipher with a key of 3.

(b) Decipher GLMTW EVI CYQQC XSS using a Caesar cipher with a key of 4.

Activity 16 (exploratory)

This activity asks you to complete a Sense program that enciphers and deciphers messages using the Caesar cipher. You will find the detailed instructions for it in the Sense activities section of the 'Study resources' page on the TU100 website.

Activity 17 (self-assessment)

How many different keys are possible with a Caesar cipher?

Monosubstitution ciphers

The Caesar cipher is the simplest example of a *monosubstitution cipher*, a substitution cipher in which each plaintext letter is replaced by the same ciphertext symbol every time it appears. With its limited number of keys, the Caesar cipher is a pretty poor cipher. If confronted with a message encrypted with a Caesar cipher with an unknown key, it's not too arduous simply to try each key in turn and see if the proposed decryption is a legible piece of text. This is an example of a *brute-force attack* to break a cipher – simply trying each of the possible keys, one after the other.

Activity 18 (exploratory)

This activity asks you to break a Caesar-enciphered message with a brute-force attack. You will find the detailed instructions for it in the Sense activities section of the 'Study resources' page on the TU100 website.

Caesar ciphers are not the only kind of monosubstitution cipher. Rather than simply sliding the ciphertext alphabet along, as happens in a Caesar cipher, we can make a stronger cipher by scrambling the cipher alphabet completely. This gives us a lot of keys. There are 26 letters we can use to encipher a, 25 to encipher b, 24 to encipher c and so on. That gives $26 \times 25 \times 24 \times \ldots \times 3 \times 2 \times 1$ possible keys, which is approximately 4.03×10^{26}. That's quite a large number.

Activity 19 (exploratory)

How long in years would it take to try all these possible keys, assuming your computer can try one million keys every second? You will probably need to use a calculator for this activity.

Comment

It would take approximately $4.03 \times 10^{26}/10^6 = 4.03 \times 10^{20}$ seconds.

Since one year is $365 \times 24 \times 60 \times 60 = 31\ 536\ 000$ seconds, this is approximately $403 \times 10^{18}/31\ 536\ 000 = 1.28 \times 10^{13}$ years. (The best guess of the age of the universe is around 13.7 billion years (13.7×10^9 years), so the total time would be approximately 1000 times the age of the universe.)

One way to create a key for a monosubstitution cipher is to use a keyword or phrase, such as 'Open University'. To form the key, take out spaces, punctuation and repeated occurrences of letters – so this converts 'Open University' to 'OPENUIVRSTY'. This phrase becomes the first part of the ciphertext alphabet in your cipher. Continue with the cipher alphabet from the last letter of the key phrase, missing out letters that have already occurred. This would give the following:

a	b	c	d	e	f	g	h	i	j	k	l	m	n	o	p	q	r	s	t	u	v	w	x	y	z
O	P	E	N	U	I	V	R	S	T	Y	Z	A	B	C	D	F	G	H	J	K	L	M	Q	W	X

Using this keyword, the message attack the forts at dawn would be encrypted as OJJOEY JRU ICGJH OJ NOMB.

The advantage of this method is that the key phrase is easier to remember than a random permutation of the alphabet, so you shouldn't need to write it down. That makes it harder for someone to steal the key. However, it reduces the number of keys available and allows an attacker to guess the key. Also, not all key phrases are equal: 'My digital life' makes a rubbish key (try it).

Given such a large number of possible keys, why are monosubstitution ciphers considered too weak for use? The answer is that codebreakers are cleverer than blindly trying each key in turn. They can also look at patterns in the ciphertext and use those to hunt for keys. One simple way of doing this is to count the number of occurrences of each letter in the ciphertext.

Frequency analysis

Natural languages, such as English, have a characteristic pattern of use of different letters. For instance, it's widely known that 'e' is the most common letter in English. Figure 9 shows the relative frequencies of letters in everyday English.

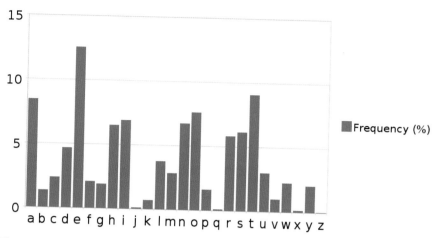

Figure 9 Letter frequencies in English

This kind of analysis is the basis of a type of popular puzzle, where you're presented with an empty crossword grid and have to fill in the letters.

Finding the relative frequencies of the letters in any sufficiently large piece of English text should result in a similar histogram. So, for example, about 8% of the letters will be 'a', about 2% of the letters will be 'b' and so on. If you analyse the letter frequencies for the ciphertext you're interested in, you can start to make guesses about the identities of the most common ciphertext letters. For example, if you notice that within the ciphertext the letter Y occurs 8% of the time then it would be worth pursuing whether ciphertext Y corresponds to plaintext a (though of course it may not – your ciphertext may be atypical).

You can also look for patterns in letter use, such as knowing that English words can contain 'ee' but not 'qq'. So if in your ciphertext you have the combination BB then it's unlikely that B is the ciphertext for q. Very often, once you've made a start on a decipherment, the rest follows.

Activity 20 (exploratory)

This activity asks you to find the letter frequencies in a piece of text. You will find the detailed instructions for it in the Sense activities section of the 'Study resources' page on the TU100 website.

Activity 21 (exploratory)

In this activity you will break a Caesar-enciphered message using frequency analysis. You will find the detailed instructions for it in the Sense activities section of the 'Study resources' page on the TU100 website.

The weakness of monoalphabetic ciphers is the one-to-one correspondence between plaintext letters and ciphertext letters, which means that a ciphertext letter occurs with the same frequency as its plaintext equivalent. This weakness is at the heart of using frequency analysis to break monosubstitution ciphers. This implies that the way to make ciphers more secure is to ensure that one plaintext letter can map to more than one ciphertext letter. There are two main ways of doing this: *homophonic ciphers* and *polyalphabetic ciphers*.

Homophonic ciphers

Homophonic ciphers try to distort the letter frequencies by assigning sets of ciphertext symbols to each plaintext letter. A plaintext letter is transformed to one of its set of ciphertext symbols; the same letter occurring in two different positions in the plaintext may be encrypted using different symbols from its assigned set. In order to undermine frequency analysis, the more common the plaintext letter the larger the set of ciphertext symbols it should be assigned. For instance, we could use the two-digit numbers 01 to 99 as ciphertext symbols. Because 'e' occurs about ten times as often as 'k' in English, we assign ten numbers to plaintext e and one number to plaintext k. So when an e occurs in the plaintext it is replaced by one of the set of ten corresponding numbers; when a k occurs it is simply always replaced by the same number. That way, when Eve comes along and tries to read the message, she's faced with a basically flat frequency histogram.

Unfortunately, a homophonic cipher still leaves other features of the plaintext intact, such as the distribution of sequences of letters (e.g. q almost always has u after it; th is common while tx is rare). Although it is tricky and time-consuming, this gives codebreakers a crack they can use to lever open the whole code. This meant that homophonic ciphers were a bit of a dead end in cryptography, despite being used for centuries.

I won't go into further details here, but you can find out more about cracking homophonic ciphers from Chapter 2 of Singh (1999).

Polyalphabetic ciphers

As I've said, a limitation of monoalphabetic ciphers – including homophonic ones – is that every letter in the plaintext is encrypted in the same way (using the same set of symbols, in the case of a homophonic cipher). This consistency allows codebreakers to apply lessons learned about one part of the ciphertext to other parts. What would be better would be to change the encryption method as we go along. That's what *polyalphabetic ciphers* do: letters in the plaintext are encrypted in a way that varies depending on their position in the plaintext. The classic example of such a cipher is the *Vigenère cipher* (see Box 5), which consists of a grid of letters with each row representing a Caesar cipher that has a different key. This is shown in Figure 10, with the plaintext alphabet in the first row.

a	b	c	d	e	f	g	h	i	j	k	l	m	n	o	p	q	r	s	t	u	v	w	x	y	z
B	C	D	E	F	G	H	I	J	K	L	M	N	O	P	Q	R	S	T	U	V	W	X	Y	Z	A
C	D	E	F	G	H	I	J	K	L	M	N	O	P	Q	R	S	T	U	V	W	X	Y	Z	A	B
D	E	F	G	H	I	J	K	L	M	N	O	P	Q	R	S	T	U	V	W	X	Y	Z	A	B	C
E	F	G	H	I	J	K	L	M	N	O	P	Q	R	S	T	U	V	W	X	Y	Z	A	B	C	D
F	G	H	I	J	K	L	M	N	O	P	Q	R	S	T	U	V	W	X	Y	Z	A	B	C	D	E
G	H	I	J	K	L	M	N	O	P	Q	R	S	T	U	V	W	X	Y	Z	A	B	C	D	E	F
H	I	J	K	L	M	N	O	P	Q	R	S	T	U	V	W	X	Y	Z	A	B	C	D	E	F	G
I	J	K	L	M	N	O	P	Q	R	S	T	U	V	W	X	Y	Z	A	B	C	D	E	F	G	H
J	K	L	M	N	O	P	Q	R	S	T	U	V	W	X	Y	Z	A	B	C	D	E	F	G	H	I
K	L	M	N	O	P	Q	R	S	T	U	V	W	X	Y	Z	A	B	C	D	E	F	G	H	I	J
L	M	N	O	P	Q	R	S	T	U	V	W	X	Y	Z	A	B	C	D	E	F	G	H	I	J	K
M	N	O	P	Q	R	S	T	U	V	W	X	Y	Z	A	B	C	D	E	F	G	H	I	J	K	L
N	O	P	Q	R	S	T	U	V	W	X	Y	Z	A	B	C	D	E	F	G	H	I	J	K	L	M
O	P	Q	R	S	T	U	V	W	X	Y	Z	A	B	C	D	E	F	G	H	I	J	K	L	M	N
P	Q	R	S	T	U	V	W	X	Y	Z	A	B	C	D	E	F	G	H	I	J	K	L	M	N	O
Q	R	S	T	U	V	W	X	Y	Z	A	B	C	D	E	F	G	H	I	J	K	L	M	N	O	P
R	S	T	U	V	W	X	Y	Z	A	B	C	D	E	F	G	H	I	J	K	L	M	N	O	P	Q
S	T	U	V	W	X	Y	Z	A	B	C	D	E	F	G	H	I	J	K	L	M	N	O	P	Q	R
T	U	V	W	X	Y	Z	A	B	C	D	E	F	G	H	I	J	K	L	M	N	O	P	Q	R	S
U	V	W	X	Y	Z	A	B	C	D	E	F	G	H	I	J	K	L	M	N	O	P	Q	R	S	T
V	W	X	Y	Z	A	B	C	D	E	F	G	H	I	J	K	L	M	N	O	P	Q	R	S	T	U
W	X	Y	Z	A	B	C	D	E	F	G	H	I	J	K	L	M	N	O	P	Q	R	S	T	U	V
X	Y	Z	A	B	C	D	E	F	G	H	I	J	K	L	M	N	O	P	Q	R	S	T	U	V	W
Y	Z	A	B	C	D	E	F	G	H	I	J	K	L	M	N	O	P	Q	R	S	T	U	V	W	X
Z	A	B	C	D	E	F	G	H	I	J	K	L	M	N	O	P	Q	R	S	T	U	V	W	X	Y
A	B	C	D	E	F	G	H	I	J	K	L	M	N	O	P	Q	R	S	T	U	V	W	X	Y	Z

Figure 10   **Vigenère cipher**

Figure 11   **Blaise de Vigenère (1523–1596)**

Box 5 The Vigenère cipher: before its time

Blaise de Vigenère (Figure 11) invented the cipher that bears his name in 1586, but it wasn't widely used until the eighteenth century. Until then cryptographers used homophonic ciphers, as they were much easier to use and sufficiently hard to break to make them useful. However, in the eighteenth century, governments started to support professional codebreakers – the so-called Black Chambers. While homophonic ciphers are normally tough enough to stop amateurs, they're not good enough to keep out teams of professionals with lots of resources. This increase in codebreaking effort forced state agents to use the Vigenère cipher.

Activity 22 (exploratory)

The final row of the Vigenère square in Figure 10 shows a Caesar cipher with a key of zero – that is, the ciphertext is the same as the plaintext. Why do you think this row is included?

Comment

If the cipher can never encrypt a letter as itself, that is a feature of the cipher that can be exploited by a codebreaker. You'll get to see how such a feature can be exploited when I talk about the breaking of the Enigma codes later in this session.

Using the Vigenère cipher involves using a key to determine which row of the square to use to encrypt a particular letter of the plaintext. For instance, let's say I want to encrypt the phrase Attack the forts at dawn with the key DIGITAL. I start by writing out the message and repeating the key above the plaintext:

Key	D	I	G	I	T	A	L	D	I	G	I	T	A	L	D	I	G	I	T	A
Plaintext	a	t	t	a	c	k	t	h	e	f	o	r	t	s	a	t	d	a	w	n
Ciphertext																				

To encrypt a letter of the plaintext, I look at the letter of the key above it. To encrypt the first a, the key letter is D. I look on the Vigenère grid for the row beginning with D. This row represents the Caesar cipher I use for this letter. I find the ciphertext letter for the plaintext a, in this case D, and that is the encryption of that letter of the plaintext. I encrypt the next letter of the plaintext the same way. The second key letter is I, so I use the row beginning with I. I find the ciphertext letter on that row that corresponds to the plaintext letter t, which is B. To encrypt the third letter, I find the row starting with G and so encrypt the t as Z. The completed ciphertext is shown below.

If you are finding this process difficult to follow, try watching the animation that's provided in the resources page associated with this part on the TU100 website.

Key	D	I	G	I	T	A	L	D	I	G	I	T	A	L	D	I	G	I	T	A
Plaintext	a	t	t	a	c	k	t	h	e	f	o	r	t	s	a	t	d	a	w	n
Ciphertext	D	B	Z	I	V	K	E	K	M	L	W	K	T	D	D	B	J	I	P	N

So, the encryption of attack the forts at dawn is DBZIVKEKMLWKTDDBJIPN. Note that the ts in the plaintext are all encrypted as different ciphertext letters, and that K in the ciphertext represents k in one place, h in another and r in yet another. The fact that the same plaintext letter is encrypted into different ciphertext letters in different parts of the ciphertext means that attacks on the cipher that try to use letter frequencies or letter relationships have no place to start.

If we choose a different key, say SAUSAGE, we end up with a different encryption: STNSCQXZEZGRZWSTXSWT, as shown below.

Key	S	A	U	S	A	G	E	S	A	U	S	A	G	E	S	A	U	S	A	G
Plaintext	a	t	t	a	c	k	t	h	e	f	o	r	t	s	a	t	d	a	w	n
Ciphertext	S	T	N	S	C	Q	X	Z	E	Z	G	R	Z	W	S	T	X	S	W	T

Activity 23 (self-assessment)

Explain why the second plaintext t is encrypted as ciphertext N above.

Activity 24 (self-assessment)

Using a Vigenère cipher and the key QUIZ (as shown below), encipher the message attack the forts at dawn.

Key	Q	U	I	Z	Q	U	I	Z	Q	U	I	Z	Q	U	I	Z	Q	U	I	Z
Plaintext	a	t	t	a	c	k	t	h	e	f	o	r	t	s	a	t	d	a	w	n
Ciphertext																				

Activity 25 (self-assessment)

Using a Vigenère cipher and the key FRED (as shown below), decipher the message XVGUJKQHXJEJJ.

Key	F	R	E	D	F	R	E	D	F	R	E	D	F
Plaintext													
Ciphertext	X	V	G	U	J	K	Q	H	X	J	E	J	J

Activity 26 (exploratory)

This activity asks you to build a Sense program that implements the Vigenère cipher. You will find the detailed instructions for it in the Sense activities section of the 'Study resources' page on the TU100 website.

Activity 27 (exploratory)

This activity asks you to decipher a Vigenère-enciphered message. You will find the detailed instructions for it in the Sense activities section of the 'Study resources' page on the TU100 website.

Because the Vigenère cipher is immune to straightforward letter frequency analysis, for a long time it was thought to be unbreakable. But once you know the trick, it's actually quite easy to crack. It just requires a fair bit of ciphertext and a bit of time. The trick was discovered by Charles Babbage (see Box 6), probably around 1854.

Box 6 Babbage and cracking the Vigenère cipher

Charles Babbage (Figure 12) is probably best known now for inventing the Difference Engine, an early mechanical calculation machine. His attempts to better it with the Analytical Engine foundered in the imprecision of Victorian manufacturing. There's a working replica of the Difference Engine in the Science Museum in London, complete with working printer.

Babbage never published his method for cracking the Vigenère cipher. The details only came out long after his death, when researchers looked through his notes. That's not too remarkable, as Babbage did lots of significant work that he didn't publish. However, he also had connections with the UK government of the day (they were heavily funding his work on the Difference and Analytical Engines). Around the time that Babbage broke the Vigenère cipher, the Crimean War against Russia started. Russia used the Vigenère cipher. Could it be that the UK government asked Babbage to keep his work secret, so that the British could read Russian military signals without suspicion? We'll probably never know, but it wouldn't be the first (or last) time that governments have kept their cryptographic advances secret.

Figure 12   Charles Babbage (1791–1871)

To understand how Babbage cracked the Vigenère cipher, take another look at the encryption of the message attack the forts at dawn using the key SAUSAGE: the ciphertext is STNSCQXZEZGRZWSTXSWT. Note that the at of attack is encrypted to ST, and that the word at is also encrypted to ST. This is because they happen to line up with the same position in the key. This is a weakness of the Vigenère cipher that allows it to be broken.

Because the key repeats throughout the message, different parts of the ciphertext will have been encrypted using the same part of the key. If the plaintext contains repeated letter sequences, it may be that they'll line up

with the same bits of the key, so you'll end up with repeated sequences of ciphertext. That's the vital insight to cracking the Vigenère cipher: repeated sequences of ciphertext letters are likely to be repeated sequences of plaintext letters encrypted with the same portions of the key.

But how does that help? If you find lots of repeated ciphertext sequences, it tells you something about the length of the key. If you find repeated sequences 18 characters apart, it suggests that 18 is some multiple of the key length. If you find other repeated sequences 66 characters apart, it suggests that 66 is also a multiple of the key length. Together, these facts suggest that the key is of length 6 (the largest common factor of 18 and 66). Looking through a long ciphertext for repeats, you'll probably get lots of indications like this about how long the key is. Once you know how long the key is, you can split the ciphertext into separate streams, each encrypted by one letter of the key. For instance, if the key is six letters long then the first, seventh, thirteenth (and so on) letters are all encrypted by the first letter of the key, Similarly, the second, eighth, fourteenth (and so on) letters are all encrypted by the second letter of the key. You're now faced with the problem of solving not one Vigenère cipher but six Caesar ciphers. And with frequency analysis, that's relatively easy.

If you have them, you can use multiple ciphertexts to perform the frequency analysis, so long as they all used the same key.

Another weakness comes from how the Vigenère cipher is normally used. To prevent the users having to write down the key (which then becomes eminently stealable or copyable), it has to be easy to remember. That means it will normally be a word or short phrase in some language. So, when you've got a candidate key that's complete gibberish, you know it's unlikely to be that one.

Activity 28 (exploratory)

This activity asks you to scan a Vigenère-enciphered message for repeated fragments of ciphertext, and hence determine the length of the key. You will find the detailed instructions for it in the Sense activities section of the 'Study resources' page on the TU100 website.

Activity 29 (exploratory)

In this activity you will use the key length you found in Activity 28, and your frequency-analysis program from Activity 21, to decipher a Vigenère-enciphered message. You will find the detailed instructions for it in the Sense activities section of the 'Study resources' page on the TU100 website.

Before moving on, take a moment to consider what you've just achieved. The Vigenère cipher was considered to be virtually unbreakable until the

start of the twentieth century – yet now that you have the right tools, you can break it in minutes. The main reason is that the task of finding repeated sequences can be done quickly by a machine. This is just one example of how the growing power of computers requires ciphers to be increasingly complex to stay ahead of the codebreakers. It's a story that's still going on.

Enigma

As I have just suggested, cryptography is one of the main forces driving computing forward. This started with the codebreaking efforts that took place in Bletchley Park during the Second World War. Out of this came the world's first programmable electronic computer, Alan Turing's work on the fundamentals of computing, and insight into the secretive world of the codebreakers.

The story revolves around two electromechanical enciphering machines used by the Germans in the Second World War, Enigma and Lorenz, which you heard about in Block 1 Part 2. Bletchley Park, in southern England, was where the ciphers of both these machines were broken. The work of the codebreakers is widely held to have shortened the war by around two years and hence saved countless lives on all sides.

Activity 30 (self-assessment)

In the resources page associated with this part on the TU100 website, you will find a video that describes the Enigma and Lorenz machines and how they work. The video also describes how the ciphers of those machines were broken, which required the development of Colossus, the world's first programmable computer.

While you watch the video, make notes on the following questions.

(a) How many possible keys did the Enigma and Lorenz machines have?

(b) Why did this mean the Germans thought that both machines generated unbreakable ciphers?

(c) What were the different parts of the machines, and how did they create a strong cipher?

(d) How did the Germans use a different key for each message?

(e) What technique did the Bletchley Park codebreakers use to crack Enigma?

(f) How did bombes check the candidate keys?

(g) Why could bombes not be used to break Lorenz messages?

2.4 Conclusion

This session introduced the basic ideas of steganography, codes and ciphers, and looked at how they can be used to protect communication from being intercepted or changed. You saw how the basic, and ancient, operations of substitution and transposition can be used to create ciphers of different strengths. You also saw how those different ciphers can easily be broken with the right ideas and sufficient computing horsepower, and you used Sense to break some quite sophisticated ciphers.

If you haven't already completed the Sense activities associated with this session then do make sure that you complete them before moving on.

This session should have helped you with the following learning outcomes.

- Describe, and explain the differences between, steganography, codes and ciphers.
- Describe, and explain the difference between, substitution and transposition in ciphers.
- Describe, and explain the difference between, monoalphabetic and polyalphabetic ciphers.
- Outline the strengths and weaknesses of a variety of ciphers.
- Use a variety of ciphers to encipher and decipher information.
- Use a variety of techniques to break simple ciphers.
- Use Sense to apply complex functions (such as encryption and decryption functions) to data represented as text and numbers.
- Use Sense to process large data sets stored as files.

In the next session, I'll look at modern ciphers and how asymmetric ciphers remove the need to send keys as well as messages. Perhaps surprisingly, this allows things such as digital signatures and safe ecommerce to exist.

Contemporary ciphers

3

The world of cryptography has moved on since Enigma in 1945, but many of the principles remain the same.

In this session you will be looking at some aspects of modern ciphers. Ciphers can now involve almost unimaginably large numbers of potential keys, and they use highly complex and sophisticated mathematical algorithms. You are not expected in TU100 to learn about the details of such ciphers; rather, I will concentrate on the principles involved and explain a little about how they contribute to the principles of information security to which you were introduced in Session 1.

3.1 Cipher strength

The use of computers has led to much stronger ciphers – needed in the face of much more determined attack. The shift to digital information has also meant that most ciphers now operate on strings of bits rather than strings of letters, allowing the ciphers to encrypt pictures, sound files and so on as well as text. This shift also means that the strength of ciphers is measured in terms of the number of bits required to store the key. Ciphers that are in common use now use keys of 256 bits or more, compared to the 10^{20} possible keys of the Enigma machine.

Activity 31 (exploratory)

How many different keys can be represented using 256 bits? How does this compare to the strength of Enigma? You will probably need to use a calculator for this activity.

Comment
256 bits gives $2^{256} = 1.16 \times 10^{77}$ possible keys. That's 10^{57} times the number of Enigma's possible keys. For comparison, 1.16×10^{77} is much more than the number of atoms in the galaxy, and within a few orders of magnitude of the number of atoms in the observable universe.

The sheer number of possible keys for modern ciphers means that they are unbreakable by brute-force attacks attempting to guess the key (so long as sufficiently strong passwords are used as keys – see Box 7).

Box 7 Password strength

Passwords (strings of letters and numbers) are often used as keys, either directly or indirectly (the correct password allowing access to a predefined cryptographic key). As passwords are strings of characters, and characters can be encoded as bits, we can talk about how many bits are needed to encode a password and hence determine how strong a key that password represents. Strong passwords need lots of bits to be resistant to brute-force attacks that guess the password.

As letters are each normally encoded with a single byte (8 bits), it's tempting to think that each letter in a password represents 8 bits of a key. However, password strength is more about how easy it is to guess the letters it consists of. If a password consists only of letters, there are only 26 choices, so each letter adds only a small amount to the strength of the password. The regularities of English further reduce the number of sensible guesses, so each letter of normal English in fact makes an even smaller contribution to the strength of the password (based on statistical analysis of English texts). Using normal dictionary words is even worse: it will take a computer milliseconds to try every word in a dictionary against your encrypted asset.

The problem of password strength is becoming more pressing as cloud computing services give cheap and easy access to vast computing resources that can be used to guess passwords. In late 2010, the first few services were appearing that use cloud computing resources to break passwords for a few pounds. This means that passwords will have to get much stronger.

There are ways to ensure that your passwords are as strong as possible, and I will talk about them in Session 4. For example, a Brazilian banker was arrested in July 2008 for suspected financial crimes. Several encrypted hard disks were seized during his arrest. After about six months, the Brazilian authorities realised they couldn't break the encryption and passed the disks over to the FBI. After a further twelve months, the data on the disks still hasn't been deciphered and looks like it never will be. With no evidence against him, the banker has been released. There is a link to more detail about this story in the resources page associated with this part on the TU100 website.

One-way functions and ciphers

Once you start to think about it, the whole notion of encryption is rather odd. How is it that enciphering is so easy, deciphering with a key is easy, but deciphering without the key is so hard?

Enciphering relies on what are known as *one-way* (or *trapdoor*) *functions*. These are mathematical processes that are easy to perform in one direction but difficult to perform in the other. Consider the function 'add two': this is easy to perform in both the forward direction (take a number, add two to it, return the result) and the reverse direction (take the result, subtract two from it, return the original number). Yet other functions don't have this property. Multiplication is one such function. If I multiply two prime numbers together, the result will be divisible by only those two numbers. For instance, $17 \times 13 = 221$, and 221 is divisible only by 13 and 17. Yet as far as we know, there isn't any general way of finding the factors of a number (those numbers that divide it exactly) other than trying lots of prime numbers, one after the other. (However, checking a possible factor is quick: just do a division and see if there's a remainder.)

DES and AES

One lesson that came from the breaking of Enigma was that ciphers using only substitution are vulnerable to *known plaintext attacks*. An attacker could guess the plaintext that corresponded to portions of the ciphertext and, if they were wrong, their errors would be limited to just those portions of the ciphertext. However, ciphers that use transposition (such as the scytale in Session 2) spread information about the plaintext throughout the ciphertext. If a cipher uses transposition then it is much more resistant to known plaintext attacks. However, substitution does more to conceal the information than transposition. That's why all modern cipher systems use both transposition and substitution. One example is the *Data Encryption Standard (DES)* and its successor, the *Advanced Encryption Standard (AES)*.

The details of DES and AES are rather involved, so I won't go into them here. The general idea is that they both use repeated transposition and substitution steps to encipher the plaintext. The aim is that the substitution stage disguises the plaintext and the transposition stage spreads it across the ciphertext. The use of multiple rounds allows the transposition stage to spread the information in the plaintext evenly across the ciphertext. It's a bit like mixing ingredients for a cake, swirling them around – but the trick is, it's done completely deterministically so that someone with the key can 'unmix' the ingredients. Ideally, a small change in the plaintext will cause changes across the whole ciphertext, meaning that any attacker has no place to start.

One way to visualise this is to encipher a picture. Take the picture in Figure 13(a), for instance. Each pixel in the picture is represented as a binary number, so it can be enciphered by substitution. Figure 13(b) shows the same picture after this stage of enciphering. It's very much changed, but you can still make out some of the edges between blocks of colour in the original. If I now apply a transposition stage to the image, you can see in Figure 13(c) that it's much more difficult to make out what the image

DES uses 56-bit keys, which are far too small to provide reliable security against attacks with modern computers. AES allows keys of up to 256 bits and is (in 2010) the accepted standard. However, as computing power becomes cheaper, expect key lengths to grow to ensure adequate security.

was about: the information about the edges has been spread across the image. By repeating the substitution and transposition stages, you can make the picture as difficult to understand as you wish.

(a)

(b)

(c)

Figure 13   Progressive substitution and transposition of an image: (a) original image; (b) with substitution applied; (c) with subsequent transposition applied

Enciphering in public

Early cipher algorithms, such as the Caesar cipher and the precise wiring of the Enigma machine, were kept secret to prevent codebreakers from understanding how the cipher worked and hence exploiting weaknesses. However, all the details of AES and similar cipher algorithms are made public (excluding individual keys, of course), yet they're still used. Why is this?

The answer is summed up in Schneier's Law, attributed to security expert Bruce Schneier by the writer and activist Cory Doctorow:

> Any person can invent a security system so clever that he or she can't imagine a way of breaking it.

This sums up the lessons from Bletchley Park and similar codebreaking institutions. A lot of the codebreaking successes of the past came from exploiting errors in either the cipher algorithm or its implementation. But the people who invented the cipher obviously couldn't see the flaws, or else they wouldn't have used it. The idea now is that if there are enough eyes looking at the implementation of an algorithm, someone will spot any possible weaknesses and they can be fixed (or that cipher discarded, if it has a fatal flaw). This benefit outweighs any advantage that may be given to codebreakers by making the cipher algorithms public.

In fact, there are so many subtle ways that an encryption algorithm can be cracked that security experts strongly advise programmers not to implement encipherment themselves, but to use code from a reputable library instead.

3.2 Asymmetric ciphers

The key distribution problem

All the ciphers you've seen so far are *symmetric ciphers*: the same key is used to encrypt and decrypt messages. You can think of these ciphers as being like a lockbox (Figure 14): if Alice puts something inside the box and locks it with the key, no one without the right key (e.g. Eve) can read or tamper with what's inside. But so long as Bob has the right key, he can open the box and get at the contents.

Figure 14 **A lockbox**

That's all well and good, but the weakness is that Alice and Bob need the same key. If Alice creates a key, how can she send it to Bob without Eve intercepting the transfer (Figure 15)? The key is just another message, and Eve can overhear everything said between Alice and Bob. If Alice creates and sends a key to Bob, Eve can take a copy of it. That means she can read anything that Alice sends to Bob. If Mallory the malicious attacker joins in, things get worse. Mallory can also take a copy of Alice's key when she sends it to Bob. Then, when Alice sends a message to Bob using that key, Mallory can intercept the message (taking it himself and preventing it from reaching Bob), open the box with his copy of Alice's key, change the message, then relock the box and send it on its way to Bob. There's no way for Bob to tell if Mallory or Eve has opened the box. This is the *key distribution problem*, and it is a major limitation of all symmetric cipher systems.

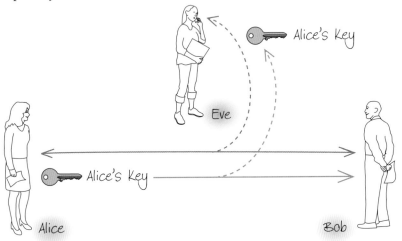

Figure 15 **The key distribution problem**

In 1977 three US researchers, Ron Rivest, Adi Shamir and Leonard Adleman, invented a robust *asymmetric cipher* (Rivest et al., 1978). Metaphorically, they'd invented a new type of lock with a very peculiar property – it has two keys. If you use one key to lock the box, you have to use the other key to unlock it (Figure 16). You can't unlock a box with the same key you used to lock it.

Rivest, Shamir and Adleman weren't the first people to invent asymmetric cryptography. That honour goes to James Ellis, Clifford Cocks and Malcolm Williamson, who worked for GCHQ, the UK government's codemakers and codebreakers. GCHQ decided to keep their discovery secret. It wasn't until the 1990s that their breakthrough was revealed.

Figure 16 **A lockbox with two keys: if the box was locked with one key then it would have to be unlocked with the other**

In reality, the two keys are numbers that are mathematically related to each other but which are such that given only one of the keys, it is impossible to work out what the other one is. The mathematical details are complex; in fact, for a long time people thought it was impossible to create a cipher that would work in this way. Thankfully, such ciphers are designed to be used without knowledge of the underlying details. However, it is important to be aware of the principles, and that is what I'll describe here.

How does this help? Well, let's say Alice creates a box and the two keys that go with it. She calls one key her *private key*, and keeps hold of it. She calls the other key her *public key*, and gives copies of it away to everyone. Alice, Bob and Eve now all have copies of Alice's public key. Bob and Eve do the same: they create a key pair, keep one of the pair private and give the other key to everyone. Overall, the position is as shown in Figure 17.

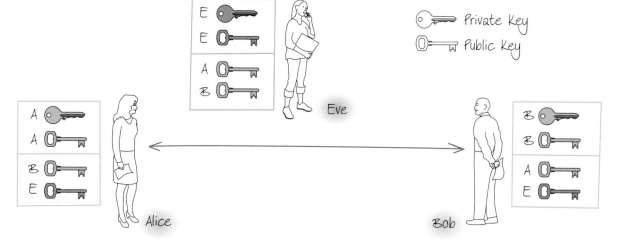

Figure 17 **Alice, Bob and Eve with keys**

Confidentiality and integrity

What happens now when Alice wants to send a message to Bob without Eve reading it (Figure 18)? She encrypts the message (locks a box) with Bob's public key. The only key that can unlock that box is the other one of the pair, which is Bob's private key. The only person who has that key is Bob: he never gave it to anyone. Now if Eve intercepts the box during

transmission, she can't unlock it because she doesn't have Bob's private key; therefore the communication is *confidential*. Mallory's in the same boat. If he somehow alters the contents of the box, he has to do so blindly, meaning that his tampering will be detectable by Bob (the decrypted message will be nonsense). This means that the communication has *integrity*.

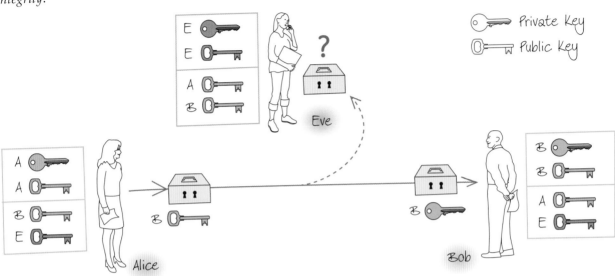

Figure 18   Exchanging messages securely using public and private keys

This shows that asymmetric ciphers can allow people to exchange messages securely without having to grapple with finding a way of exchanging keys securely – but it gets better. As you may remember, in Session 1 I said that we want messages to be *authenticated* (i.e. so we know who sent them) and non-repudiable (i.e. so the sender can't later deny that he or she sent them). Asymmetric ciphers solve both these problems.

Authentication

If Alice wants to send a message to Bob so he will be convinced that it really came from her, she can encrypt the message with her private key. This means that anyone who holds Alice's public key (i.e. everyone) can decrypt and read the message. On the face of it, that doesn't gain anyone anything. But if Alice sends both the plaintext of the message and the message encrypted with her private key, that says something about the authenticity of the message. When Bob receives the message, he can read the plaintext. He can also decrypt the ciphertext with Alice's public key. If the two messages are the same, he can be confident that the message really came from Alice. In other words, the message is *authenticated* as coming from Alice.

To see why Bob can be confident of the identity of the sender, let's see what happens if Eve sends him a message purporting to come from Alice. Eve will create the message, encrypt it with her own private key, and send

the plaintext and ciphertext to Bob. Bob will read the message, see it supposedly comes from Alice and decrypt the ciphertext with Alice's public key. He will end up with gibberish. That tells him that the ciphertext was not created with Alice's private key, and therefore he can't be sure that it really did come from Alice.

Non-repudiation

Non-repudiation of messages works similarly. As a security measure, Alice's private key will only work if Alice provides a password when she wants to encrypt or decrypt a message. (This means that even if Eve manages to steal Alice's private key, she'll have to find Alice's password to use it – if it's a strong password, that will take centuries.) If Bob receives a message that was encrypted by Alice's private key, he knows that someone must have provided Alice's password to use her private key. That person must be Alice, so Alice must have known that she was sending the message. This means that Bob can use the fact that the message was encrypted with Alice's private key as evidence that Alice did send the message, even if she later denies it.

Digital signatures

If Alice wants to make sure that only Bob can read the message, and have Bob be sure that the message really did come from her, she can use two encryption stages (Figure 19). First, she encrypts the message with her own private key (to sign it). Then, she bundles the encrypted and plaintext versions of her message together, and encrypts the whole bundle with Bob's public key. When Bob receives the message, he can undo all the stages to get to the original message, with the assurance that it came from Alice and that Eve didn't read it.

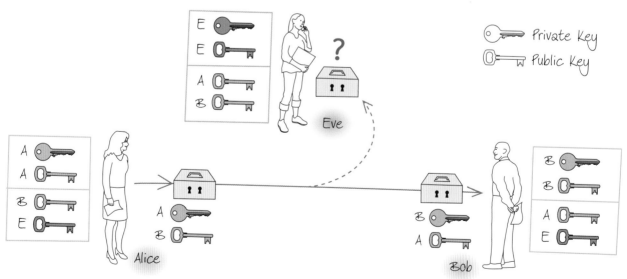

Figure 19   Two-stage encryption process

This combination of authentication and non-repudiation is the same as conferred by a written signature on a piece of paper. Therefore, asymmetric ciphers can be used to create *digital signatures*. Such digital signatures have the same weight in law as written signatures. In effect, when Alice uses her private key to encrypt a message, she is 'signing' the message.

In practice all the encryption, and the bundling and unbundling of messages, is done automatically by Alice's and Bob's email programs. A similar process occurs with using digital certificates to authenticate secure websites, which I will discuss below.

Activity 32 (self-assessment)

There are several desirable features of information security: confidentiality, integrity, accessibility, authentication and non-repudiation. Which of these are assured for Bob when Alice signs a message with her private key and encrypts it with Bob's public key?

3.3 Trusting keys

Man-in the-middle attacks

Let's take things a bit further and say that Eve can control all the communication between Alice and Bob. Alice and Bob create their own key pairs and publish their own public keys, but Eve prevents Alice and Bob from receiving copies of each other's public keys. Instead, Eve creates two further asymmetric key pairs. She gives one public key to Alice, saying it's from Bob; she gives the other public key to Bob, saying it's from Alice. Now when Alice sends a message to Bob, she will use the fake-Bob public key that Eve provided. Eve can intercept the message, read it using her fake-Bob private key, re-encrypt it with her genuine copy of Bob's public key and send the message on to Bob. When Bob decrypts the message (with his own private key), it all checks out so he's confident that Eve hasn't read the message. The same thing happens if Alice signs her message with her private key: Eve intercepts the message, undoes Alice's signing, then re-signs with the fake-Alice private key. When Bob receives the message, he checks the signature with what he thinks is Alice's public key, and so he is confident that the message came from Alice. This is known as a *man-in-the-middle attack* (see Figure 20). What's to stop Eve doing this?

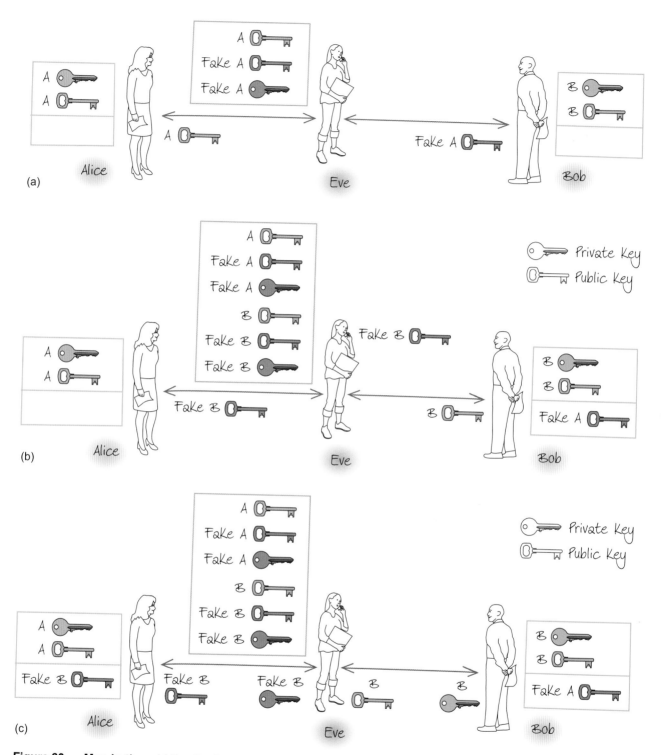

Figure 20 Man-in-the-middle attack: (a) Eve intercepts Alice's public key and passes a fake-Alice public key to Bob; (b) Eve intercepts Bob's public key and passes a fake-Bob public key to Alice; (c) Eve can now read all messages between Alice and Bob

The short answer is, nothing. If Eve really does control all communication between Alice and Bob, there's no way around it. The best Alice and Bob can hope for is that they can find some way of communicating that Eve can't control. Then Bob can ask Alice if the public key he has is really her key, and vice versa. This is generally done in a face-to-face meeting. Bob can also check that the person he's talking to really is Alice, often by checking passports and other forms of identification. (This isn't the same as the key distribution problem, as neither Alice nor Bob cares if Eve overhears their conversation. They're only discussing public keys, after all.)

Digital certificates

Let's now say that Charlie wants to talk to Alice. Charlie can get hold of something that purports to be Alice's public key, but for some reason he can't contact Alice directly to verify it. What can Charlie do? Well, if he trusts Bob, perhaps he can ask Bob to vouch for the authenticity of Alice's key. Bob can vouch for Alice's key by signing it: cryptographic keys are just data, after all, and so can be signed by encrypting them with a private key. Bob should sign Alice's key only when he's confident that it really does belong to Alice. Bob can then make this signed key public so the whole world knows that he thinks Alice's key is valid. Now when Charlie comes across Alice's public key, he'll see that it's been signed by Bob. If Charlie trusts Bob to sign keys only when it's warranted, Charlie should now trust that Alice's key really belongs to her and he can use it to send secure messages to Alice (see Figure 21). Keys that have been signed for their authenticity are called *digital certificates*.

Charlie's trust in Alice's key depends on how much he trusts Bob. Depending on exactly who Bob is, there are two different ways of spreading authority: direct trust and webs of trust.

Direct trust

This approach has everyone trusting Bob directly. In Figure 22 the direct trust relationship is shown by a blue line, while vouching for a third party is shown by a dashed orange line. Thus Bob trusts Alice directly and is willing to vouch for her (sign her key); Charlie trusts Alice because he trusts Bob directly (and so trusts Bob's judgement about other people), and he knows Bob vouches for Alice.

It's unlikely that lots of people are going to trust Bob directly if he's just an individual. But if Bob is a large, government-regulated security organisation, that's quite different. Such organisations are called *certificate authorities (CAs)* or *trusted third parties (TTPs)*, and for a fee they will sign public keys such as those associated with commercial websites. Figure 23 shows two CAs, CA1 and CA2.

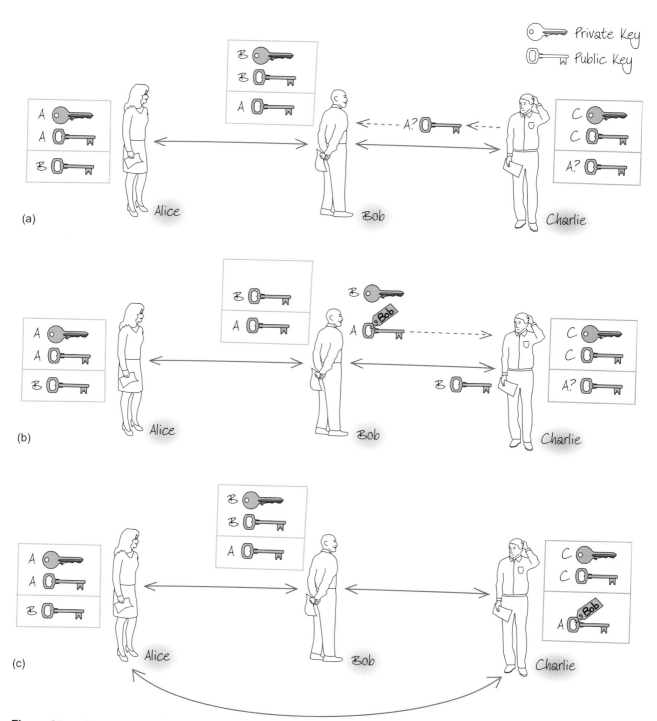

Figure 21 Signed keys: (a) Charlie asks Bob whether the key he has is really Alice's public key; (b) Bob signs the key to verify that it belongs to Alice; (c) Charlie can now send secure messages to Alice

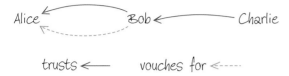

Figure 22   Direct trust

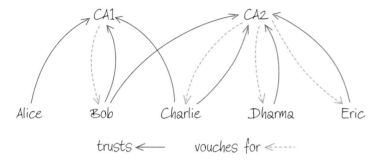

Figure 23   Trust in a CA-based system: Alice accepts Bob's key, Bob accepts Charlie's, Dharma's and Eric's keys, and no one accepts Alice's key

Activity 33 (self-assessment)

Using Figure 23, answer the following questions.

(a) Who accepts Charlie's key?

(b) Whose keys does Charlie accept?

(c) Whose keys does Alice accept?

Web browsers come with the public keys of a number of CAs installed in them. When you visit a secure website, your browser downloads the site's certificate. If it's signed with a key from a CA your browser knows about, the certificate is accepted. If not, your browser complains.

To enable secure communication with a website, your browser negotiates with that website over what encryption method to use. Your browser generates a key for this session, encrypts the session key with the site's public key, and sends it to the site. You can then communicate using the session key to keep everything secure.

The direct trust model is fine so long as the CA remains trustworthy, but some CAs have exhibited suspicious behaviour. For instance, Etisalat is a mobile phone operator in the United Arab Emirates that has attempted to introduce spyware onto Blackberry devices. Etisalat is also a CA, automatically trusted by most web browsers in the world. The suspicion is that if Etisalat can't be trusted, it can perform a man-in-the-middle attack against users on its own network. This attack would work because, at

present, browsers don't normally report which CA is authenticating a secure website, and all CAs are regarded as being equally trusted.

Web of trust

The other possible approach is a *web of trust*, as illustrated in Figure 24. In this model, no one person is responsible for authenticating all keys. Instead, individuals sign each other's keys as they individually trust each other. Keys can be signed by multiple people, increasing the chance that a key you come across is signed by someone you personally trust. This model is also easy to set up: several communities have created their own webs of trust for their own use. However, it does take some effort, which – combined with the often unfriendly user interfaces of many encryption systems – is a significant reason why the routine encryption of emails by users via this model hasn't become commonplace.

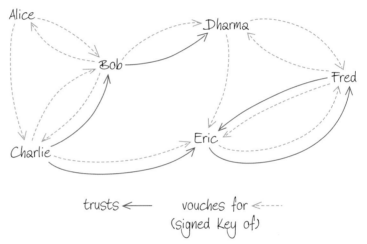

Figure 24   Trust in a web of trust: Alice accepts Bob's and Charlie's keys only, Bob accepts everyone's key, Dharma accepts Eric's and Fred's keys, and Eric accepts Fred's and Dharma's keys

Activity 34 (self-assessment)

Using the web of trust in Figure 24, answer the following questions.

(a) Whose keys does Charlie accept?

(b) Who accepts Charlie's key?

(c) Whose keys does Fred accept?

(d) Who accepts Fred's key?

Activity 35 (exploratory)

What are the advantages and disadvantages of a trust model based on CAs versus one based on a web of trust?

Comment

A model based on CAs means that trust is easy to establish. If Bob is acting as a CA then every time Charlie wants to communicate with a new person, he just needs to check with Bob. The disadvantage is that if Bob goes away or starts to give false assurances, all Charlie's communication becomes suspect.

In contrast, a web of trust model means that Charlie doesn't have to trust any one person. If Bob becomes suspect, Charlie can find someone else to vouch for the people he talks to. On the other hand, navigating a web of trust is much more time-consuming, as you have to find and verify more people as well as sign keys yourself.

3.4 Limits of cryptography

The creative use of cryptography can do a lot to keep us all secure online. Cryptography can ensure that our communication and data storage is and remains confidential. It can alert us to changes in stored or transmitted data, ensuring integrity. Authentication, providing reliable methods of checking the identity of people and organisations online, has great potential to reduce fraud and other crimes.

As well as authenticating people, asymmetric ciphers can be used to authenticate organisations and servers, thus reducing the risks of inadvertently downloading malware. Authenticating email servers can also reduce email spam (the *bots* that send much of this spam wouldn't authenticate, so your email system would refuse to accept any mail from them). So cryptography would seem to offer many benefits to the internet.

However, one of the factors in the explosive and vibrant growth of the internet has been the ability of anyone to set up a server without anyone else's permission: if all servers had to be authenticated with one of a few trusted CAs, there would have been much fewer of them in operation. With fewer servers, the internet would not have taken off as rapidly as it did. Perhaps spam is the price we pay for allowing innovation online. This position is argued in an article by Cory Doctorow (2005) entitled *All Complex Ecosystems Have Parasites*, a link to which is provided on the resources page associated with this part on the TU100 website.

Cryptography is only one tool in an arsenal of security measures and, like all tools, it's useless if it's not used properly. The history of security (not just computer and information security) is littered with examples where good security measures were rendered useless, either by flawed implementations (such as Enigma) or by people just deciding the security measures were getting in the way and bypassing them. All the cryptography in the world won't help you if you run software from an

unreliable source or give your bank details to a stranger. In fact, the history of data loss and data theft is littered with examples in which cryptographically secure methods of storing data were bypassed as a result of people either not using them properly or using easy-to-guess passwords.

3.5 Conclusion

This session continued the story of the previous session. First, you learned how substitution and transposition are still used as the basis of modern ciphers, just with much larger keys. You also saw how ciphers are hampered by the key distribution problem and how that is solved by using asymmetric ciphers. That also brought up questions about trust and identity and the notion of digital signatures and certificates.

This session should have helped you with the following learning outcomes.

*   Describe the basic principles of information security and show how they apply to a range of situations.
*   Describe, and explain the difference between, substitution and transposition in ciphers.
*   Describe, and explain the difference between, symmetric and asymmetric ciphers.
*   Describe the concept of digital signatures and digital certificates, and how they can be used to provide assurance of authenticity and non-repudiation.
*   Understand the notion of a one-way function and how ciphers can be based on such functions.

As you'll recall from Session 1, cryptography is just one part of information security. The next session will show you some simple but effective steps to follow in order to keep your information and your computer safe and secure.

Security for the individual

4

Back in Session 1, you found out a lot about information security and the threats to it. You're probably bombarded by messages from all sides about the dreadful things that can go wrong and what you should do about it. But really, you can prevent just about all security threats from materialising with just a few simple steps. Roughly in order of priority, these are as follows:

- Take backups – and make sure they work.
- Install all software updates.
- Use strong passwords, once.
- Use good anti-malware tools.
- Don't run as administrator.
- Suspect incoming messages.
- Encrypt data.
- Don't reveal personal information.

I'll now expand on what each of these means.

> This advice isn't aimed at experts. If you're a computer expert, you may have more ideas on what people can do to stay safe.

4.1 Take backups – and make sure they work

Frankly, the most likely breach of information security that you'll experience is you deleting the wrong file (I've done it many a time). Beyond that, things such as hard disk failures and house fires can also destroy your information. There's not much you can do to prevent that, but you can ensure that you don't suffer too much as a result. Make sure you take backups of all your information, regularly, and make sure the backups work. Store backups in different places, so a fire or a flood won't get them all: portable hard disks are sufficiently cheap and robust to be a good choice.

Note that making sure the backups work is not an optional step. Pixar Studios didn't manage it, and as a result they almost lost the film *Toy Story 2*: several person-decades of work.

At the time of writing (2010), bandwidth and storage isn't *quite* plentiful enough for me to make regular backups of all my stuff to a server in the cloud. But in a few years I'm sure I'll be doing that, with suitable encryption to ensure the data is confidential.

> I'm sure you've heard this advice about backups plenty of times before. But it's funny that no matter how many times they hear it, no one ever takes it seriously until they've irrevocably lost something important. Then, and only then, do people seem to get the message. I hope you're the exception to the rule.

4.2   Install all software updates

Most malware gets onto your machine, and does damage, by exploiting specific flaws in some software. As soon as these flaws become apparent, the software creator will fix them and issue an update. Very often, security investigators will find and fix the flaws before they're widely known and hence before they're exploited. Therefore, when you get a message that there's an update available for some piece of software on your computer, install it. Well-patched machines are remarkably resilient to purely technical attacks.

Do make sure you update everything that asks. Online criminals are very good at finding the most convoluted routes into your PC. Software updates close those holes, and the software only accepts updates from known sources.

4.3   Use strong passwords, once

Just about every website you sign on to requires a password. If your passwords are easily guessable, you are effectively giving attackers open access to your accounts. If your passwords are along the lines of 'password', '123' or 'letmein', they won't even need to use their automatic password-breaking tools. This is especially true when people don't change the default passwords that come with pieces of equipment such as broadband routers.

Most password attacks happen when a website gets compromised and someone gets a copy of the user list. The passwords are typically encoded with a cryptographic hash function (see Box 8) before storing, but the attacker can generate lots of possible passwords, hash them and see whether any of them match a stored one. Attackers always start with dictionary words and variations thereof, as most passwords are normal words.

Box 8 Cryptographic hash functions

A cryptographic hash function is a one-way, keyless cipher. Once some text has been hashed (i.e. encrypted using such a cipher), it's effectively impossible to recover the original text from the hashed result, and no two pieces of text should hash to the same result. When you set your password for a site, what you enter is hashed and stored. When you later give your password to gain access to an account, what you enter is hashed again and compared to the stored hashed value. If they match, the passwords that generated the hashes must have been the same.

So, strong passwords – long, non-dictionary words that are not easily guessable – are vital. The other thing to remember is to use a different password for every account. The majority of cases in which someone's password has been compromised have occurred when an attacker has cracked someone's password on a low-value, low-security site, and that user used the same password for another, higher-value site (see Figure 25). The attacker either knows or guesses the target's username on the high-value site and tries the cracked password on it.

But how do you make passwords that are strong and unique? Longer is better: passwords should be at least 12 characters long, but making them 30 or more is better. One way to create non-dictionary passwords that are easily memorable is to use the initial letters of words in a phrase or saying you know well, such as a line of a favourite song.

A better alternative is to generate purely random passwords. Tables 3(a) and (b) show one way to do this. Use a die or a coin to pick one of the tables, then roll two dice to pick a character from the table. You'll soon be using passwords like #A£kpz$DkTC14KxhiTLm and gykOs£RAznD0&XImIq7^, which are unlikely to be in any dictionary.

Table 3

(a)

Red die		White die					
		1	2	3	4	5	6
	1	a	b	c	d	e	f
	2	g	h	i	j	k	l
	3	m	n	o	p	q	r
	4	s	t	u	v	w	x
	5	y	z	0	1	2	3
	6	4	5	6	7	8	9

(b)

Red die		White die					
		1	2	3	4	5	6
	1	A	B	C	D	E	F
	2	G	H	I	J	K	L
	3	M	N	O	P	Q	R
	4	S	T	U	V	W	X
	5	Y	Z	!	£	$	%
	6	^	&	*	@	#	~

If you use a strong password for a particular site or service, you don't need to change it often. You will frequently come across advice that passwords should be changed every few weeks or months, in order to limit the window of opportunity that an attacker has to cause damage once they have access to your account. This assumes that you won't notice any damage they're doing at first. However, most attackers will simply do what they want to with your account as soon as they have access, and you'll notice quickly. As soon as you think that an account has been compromised, or that someone could conceivably have sneaked a peek at your password, change it immediately.

Figure 25   The dangers of password reuse

Remembering passwords

Given the recommendation that you use different, strong passwords, you might be concerned at how you're going to remember them all.

Firstly, you may not need to remember all of them, as most browsers now remember your passwords for you. If you use that facility, remember to set a master password to prevent an attacker from gaining access to your accounts if they steal your laptop. That master password is one you must commit to memory.

This advice – storing passwords on your PC – makes sense if you always use the same PC. If you use several computers (e.g. a work machine, a home machine and a smart phone) and trust them all, you can just type the passwords into each machine.

If several people use the same PC (such as family members using a common PC at home), give everyone their own account to use (see Section 4.5 for details).

If, on the other hand, you use public PCs – such as in libraries or cyber-cafés – then frankly, there's not much you can do. The problem with those PCs is that any prior user could have installed any type of malware (either accidentally or deliberately), which could affect your session. That malware could do things like use a *keylogger* to record all your keystrokes (including the passwords you type in) and send them to a hacker's computer.

Personally, I wouldn't trust any public-use PC at all. I most certainly wouldn't do anything sensitive on it, such as online banking. And if you do use a public PC then please, please, please make sure you log out of any websites you use and close the browser when you've finished. You don't want the next person who comes along to hit the Back button on the browser and get back into your account.

If you have a choice between writing down a complicated password and using a simple but easily memorable one, use the complex password. If you have to write down passwords, remember that they are as valuable as cash and should be protected as such. Keep them somewhere secure (such as with your financial details, or in your wallet or purse) and don't list which password is for which service. Put several spurious passwords on the same piece of paper, and add a few characters to the beginning and end of the real password. You might also want to ensure that your next of kin can recover your passwords should the worst happen to you.

You shouldn't reveal your passwords to anyone, especially people who phone or email you purporting to be from various organisations. The password you use to access your email is probably the most important one, as most 'reset my password' mechanisms work via email.

4.4   Use good anti-malware tools

As you hopefully discovered in Session 1, malware can get onto your PC from many different sources.

A virus is just one kind of malware, but in fact 'anti-virus' tools are actually general anti-malware tools. They detect and, in many cases, remove all sorts of malware. Find a good one (there are plenty of reviews online; don't discount free or open source tools just because they're free). As well as checking incoming messages, most of these tools will also keep an eye on the contents of your computer's storage in case any malware sneaks through.

Most systems detect malware in two ways: they have a list of known malware 'signatures' (fragments of code contained in malware) that can be detected in files and messages, and they monitor programs for 'suspicious behaviour' such as writing to sensitive files. Whatever anti-malware tool you use, make sure it has regular updates so that it's aware of the latest threats out there.

Many websites will run automatic tests of your firewall setting for you. Search online for 'port scanning'.

Another protective tool is a firewall, which you learned about in Block 1. Firewalls stand between your computer and the outside world, preventing other computers from connecting to yours. Generally, open 'ports' are like open doors for an attacker to get to the data on your computer. Firewalls close those ports.

4.5   Don't run as administrator

When malware infects your computer, it installs or modifies files on it. Normally, the operating system prevents people from modifying files they're not supposed to. However, users with administrator rights can modify any files anywhere. If you're logged in as an administrator, all programs you run (including malware installers) will have those rights too. That makes it easy for malware to install itself. If you don't need to install software often (and most of the time you won't), you don't need those rights so won't miss them if you don't have them.

Create one user account for each person who uses your computer. Make sure none of them have administrator rights. Make sure the administrator account is separate but available for when you need it.

Having separate accounts for each user also has the benefit that each user can have their own application settings, desktop layout, bookmarks and so on, without interference from other users of the machine. All modern operating systems have a quick 'switch user' facility, so it's easy for everyone to use their own account.

Finally, make sure the administrator user account has a strong password.

4.6   Suspect incoming messages

With all your software updated and anti-malware tools and a firewall running, your computer is pretty resistant to direct technological attacks. However, that's the easy bit. The weakest point in your security infrastructure is you. You have to make sure that your own actions don't compromise the security features you've set up.

The first thing to remember is not to open any attachments to emails unless you're very sure of their provenance. Attachments from people you don't know are definitely out. Even attachments from people you do know can't automatically be trusted, as one of the first things that malware does is email copies of itself to everyone in the affected person's address book.

You also need to be aware of phishing attempts. As you learned in Block 1, links embedded in email messages can take you to sites that look legitimate but aren't. If you type your log-in details into a form on a page that isn't really your bank's website, you can expect a larger overdraft soon. If you need to visit a site, type the address yourself or use a bookmark you created.

No legitimate representative of any organisation will ever ask you for your password. If you do get asked, report it.

4.7   Encrypt data

Modern operating systems will offer to encrypt your hard disk when you install them. Take them up on that offer, especially for portable computers. Encrypt the whole disk, not just specific files. (Operating systems tend to store temporary copies of files in various places and don't delete those copies until the space is needed for something else.) Removable media should also be encrypted: systems such as TrueCrypt are virtually transparent to use, so there's no excuse to forgo the protection they offer. That way, when you leave your laptop on a train, or a memory stick falls out of your pocket, none of your information is compromised.

Remember to note the password you used when encrypting. If you lose the password, you lose all the data.

4.8   Don't reveal personal information

Finally, it's worth recalling what you learned from the previous part about the perils of identity fraud, or even just the dangers that can come from someone 'joining the dots' across your different online personas. Be aware that information you post in one place can, usually quite easily, be joined up with information in another place. Neither on its own is a problem,

but when combined it can be an issue. Just be careful about how much you reveal.

4.9 Conclusion

This session should have helped you with the following learning outcomes.

- Identify the vulnerabilities of, and threats to, a range of information assets.

- Propose and implement simple actions to increase information security for individuals or small teams.

Summary

This part has been about information security. You've looked at the information assets you have and need to protect, and the threats that could compromise those assets. Then you moved on to look at cryptography, a very powerful set of techniques for keeping information secure. You learned about a variety of techniques used to encipher information, and about their weaknesses. By learning how to break various ciphers, you gained an insight into the ongoing arms race between codemakers and codebreakers. Finally, you learned some simple techniques to keep yourself and your information safe online.

Once you have completed all the online activities associated with this part you can move on to Part 4, which directly follows this part in the book. It will look at data protection from a different perspective – that of the law – as it considers some issues around digital rights management and copyright in the modern world of information sharing.

Answers to self-assessment activities

Activity 1

(a) For Ma.gnolia, the problem was accessibility: Ma.gnolia's staff and users could not access their data. However, confidential data remained secure, and no one was misled by changed data.

(b) For Twitter, the problem wasn't so much accessibility (Twitter's information was still accessible to many users) as integrity; that is, the integrity of the DNS records, which no longer pointed correctly to the Twitter website. However, no personal information was exposed so there was no breach of confidentiality.

Activity 10

The call's existence isn't hidden, so it's not steganography. The range of messages that can be sent is also small, as the calls are prearranged. That means it's not a cipher. The calls are a code, as they take the form of a set of prearranged signals that have no particular information content themselves.

Activity 12

You should use a table of three rows and $20 \div 3$ (rounded up) = 7 columns, filled out like this:

a	t	t	a	c	k	t
h	e	f	o	r	t	s
a	t	d	a	w	n	

which gives an enciphered message of

AHATETTFDAOACRWKTNTS

Activity 15

(a) The enciphered message is L OLNH VDXVDJHV.

(b) The deciphered message is chips are yummy too.

Activity 17

The total number of different keys is 25. Although an offset of 26 is possible, this will simply make the ciphertext the same as the plaintext, which is less than useful for concealing a message.

Activity 23

To encrypt the second t, the key letter is U. We look on the Vigenère grid (Figure 10) for the row beginning with U. This row represents the Caesar

cipher we use for t. We use this row to find the ciphertext letter for the plaintext t; in this case it is N.

Activity 24

To encipher the first a, use the key letter Q. Find the row in the Vigenère grid (Figure 10) that starts with Q and go across until you're under the plaintext a. The letter you read off (Q) is the ciphertext letter.

To encipher the first t, use the key letter U. Find the row in the Vigenère grid that starts with U and go across until you're under the plaintext t. The letter you read off (N) is the ciphertext letter.

To encipher the second t, use the key letter I. Find the row in the Vigenère grid that starts with I and go across until you're under the plaintext t. The letter you read off (B) is the ciphertext letter.

Continue doing this for the entire plaintext message. You should end up with the following solution:

Key	Q	U	I	Z	Q	U	I	Z	Q	U	I	Z	Q	U	I	Z	Q	U	I	Z
Plaintext	a	t	t	a	c	k	t	h	e	f	o	r	t	s	a	t	d	a	w	n
Ciphertext	Q	N	B	Z	S	E	B	G	U	Z	W	Q	J	M	I	S	T	U	E	M

Activity 25

To decipher the first letter, find the row in Figure 10 that starts with F and go along until you find X. The plaintext letter at the top of this column is s, so the first plaintext letter is s.

To decipher the second letter, find the row that starts with R and go along until you find V. The plaintext letter at the top of this column is e, so the second plaintext letter is e.

Continue until you've deciphered the whole message, as shown below.

Key	F	R	E	D	F	R	E	D	F	R	E	D	F
Plaintext	s	e	c	r	e	t	m	e	s	s	a	g	e
Ciphertext	X	V	G	U	J	K	Q	H	X	J	E	J	J

Activity 30

(a) The Enigma had 10^{20} possible keys. The Lorenz had 10^{23} keys, a thousand times more.

(b) The number of possible keys meant that any brute-force attack to find the key being used would take an unfeasibly long time.

(c) Both machines used rotors to change the substitution for each letter in the message. Enigma used a choice of fixed rotors and an additional plugboard. Lorenz used configurable pins on its rotors.

(d) Different keys were generated by putting the rotors in a different position before enciphering each message. The rotor positions used were transmitted with the message.

(e) The codebreakers used *known plaintext attacks*, where they guessed the content of enciphered messages and used that to determine the Enigma machine settings.

(f) Constraints on the keys were described as menus, which were wired into the bombes. The bombes checked all the possible rotor settings to see which matched those constraints.

(g) The increased complexity of Lorenz meant that the mechanical bombes weren't fast enough. Electronic circuits in Colossus were needed.

Activity 32

Alice signing the message with her private key gives the message authentication and non-repudiation. Encrypting it with Bob's public key gives it confidentiality and integrity.

Activity 33

(a) Bob, Dharma and Eric will accept Charlie's key. Only CA2 vouches for Charlie, and Alice doesn't trust CA2.

(b) Charlie accepts Bob's, Dharma's and Eric's keys. Charlie trusts both CAs, and therefore accepts keys that either CA vouches for.

(c) Alice accepts only Bob's key. Alice trusts only CA1, and that CA vouches only for Bob.

Activity 34

(a) Charlie accepts the keys of the people whose keys he signed (Bob and Eric, both of whom he also trusts to vouch for others' keys), and the people whose keys they signed (Alice, Dharma and Fred).

(b) Charlie's key is accepted by the people who signed his key (Alice and Bob), and the people who trust Alice and Bob to vouch for others' keys (no one further).

(c) Fred accepts the keys of the people whose keys he signed (Dharma and Eric). Fred doesn't trust Dharma to vouch for anyone else's key. He trusts Eric to do that, but Eric hasn't vouched for anyone except Fred himself.

(d) Fred's key is accepted by the people who signed his key (Dharma and Eric), and the people who trust Dharma and Eric to vouch for others' keys (Bob and Charlie respectively).

Glossary

accessibility When applied to data, ensuring that the information is available to those who should have access to it.

adware Malware that affects the operation of a computer by presenting the user with adverts in pop-up windows.

Advanced Encryption Standard (AES) A modern **symmetric cipher**.

Alice A standard actor in cryptographic examples. Normally, Alice wants to send a message to Bob without Eve or Mallory interfering.

asymmetric cipher A cipher in which one key is used to encipher and a different key is used to decipher. Contrast with **symmetric cipher**.

authentication The act of checking that the identity of a person (or entity) is what they claim it to be.

Bob A standard actor in cryptographic examples. Normally, Bob wants to receive a message from Alice without Eve or Mallory interfering.

bot One computer in a **botnet**.

botnet A collection of computers controlled by someone other than their nominal owners. Often the individual computers are running malware that makes them run this way, with the owners of the computers unaware that they are being controlled remotely.

brute-force attack A method of breaking a cipher by trying all possible keys.

certificate authority (CA) An organisation trusted to generate certificates only for keys that belong to who they say they do, usually for a fee.

CIA Abbreviation for confidentiality, integrity and accessibility, the principles behind information security.

cipher An algorithm that takes plaintext and a key and produces ciphertext. Also known as an *encryption function*.

ciphertext Information that has been encrypted.

code A way of securely communicating by using a few prearranged signals. Contrast with **steganography** and **ciphers**.

confidentiality When applied to data, an assurance that the data is accessible only to those who are authorised to access it.

countermeasure In terms of information security, something that mitigates a **vulnerability** or a **threat**.

cryptography The science of codes and ciphers.

Data Encryption Standard (DES) A cipher that was widely used, but became obsolete when affordable computers became sufficiently powerful to defeat it. It has been superseded by the **Advanced Encryption Standard (AES)**, which uses a longer key.

decrypt To recover an original plaintext message from ciphertext. Also referred to as *decipher*.

denial of service (DoS) attack An attack on a computer system that makes it unavailable for legitimate users.

digital certificate A public key that has been digitally signed as belonging to the person who claims to own it.

digital signature Sometimes used to mean a scanned copy of a person's handwritten signature; more properly, digital data that can be used for purposes equivalent to those of handwritten signatures, such as authentication and non-repudiation.

distributed denial of service (DDoS) attack A denial of service attack that is launched from a number of sites, often in the form of a **botnet**.

encrypt To transform a message from plaintext to ciphertext. Also referred to as *encipher*.

Eve A standard actor in cryptographic examples. Normally, Eve wants to eavesdrop on a message from Alice to Bob.

homophonic cipher A cipher where each letter can be enciphered in many ways, with the most common letters having more possible encipherments. Contrast with **monosubstitution** and **polyalphabetic** ciphers.

integrity When applied to data, an assurance that the data is able to be changed only by those who are authorised to modify it.

key The information used, in conjunction with an algorithm, to encrypt or decrypt a message.

key distribution problem The problem of sending a cryptographic key from originator to recipient without anyone else intercepting it. If the key can be sent securely, why not send the messages by the same route?

keylogger A piece of malware that logs all keystrokes on a keyboard, including usernames and passwords. They are then often sent to the malware owner.

known plaintext attack An attack against a cipher where both the plaintext and the ciphertext are known, giving the attacker information about the cipher.

Mallory A standard actor in cryptographic examples. Normally, Mallory wants to modify a message from Alice to Bob for some malicious purpose.

malware   Malicious software designed to enter computer systems without the knowledge of the owner. Includes viruses, trojans and worms.

man-in-the-middle attack   A situation in which an attacker controls the communication channel used by people wanting to communicate and uses that to intercept and perhaps modify all their communication.

monosubstitution cipher   A substitution-based cipher where every letter is enciphered in the same way each time it appears. Contrast with **homophonic** and **polyalphabetic** ciphers.

non-repudiation   The act of preventing a person from denying something they have done. For example, the presence of a valid signature on a cheque should prevent the person who wrote the cheque from denying they wrote it.

one-way function   A mathematical process that is easy to perform in one direction but difficult to perform in the other, such as the multiplication of two numbers compared to finding the factors of a number. Also known as a *trapdoor function*.

phishing   The act of sending a hoax email message that aims to persuade users to disclose private information such as credit card details or pin numbers. Hoax websites are also used as part of these scams.

plaintext   Information that is to be encrypted.

polyalphabetic cipher   A cipher where the method used to encipher each letter depends on its position in the plaintext. Contrast with **monosubstitution** and **homophonic** ciphers.

private key   The key in an asymmetric cipher that is kept secret by its owner.

public key   The key in an asymmetric cipher that is distributed widely by its owner.

spam   Unsolicited (junk) email. Spammers typically send an email to a distribution list consisting of millions of 'harvested' email addresses. More generally, unsolicited mass advertising.

spyware   Malware that spies on users, passing the information to the malware owner.

steganography   The art of securing a message by concealing its presence or existence. Contrast with **codes** and **ciphers**.

substitution   A method of enciphering by replacing each portion (often a letter) of the message with its enciphered equivalent. Contrast with **transposition**.

symmetric cipher   A cipher in which the same key is used to encipher and decipher. Contrast with **asymmetric cipher**.

threat In terms of information security, some danger that can exploit a **vulnerability**.

trusted third party (TTP) A person or organisation trusted to generate certificates only for keys that belong to who they say they do.

transposition A method of enciphering by rearranging pieces of the message. Contrast with **substitution**.

vulnerability In terms of information security, a point at which there is potential for a security breach.

web of trust A method of conferring trust that involves individuals signing each other's keys rather than relying on a few public certificate authorities.

References

Doctorow, C. (2005) *All Complex Ecosystems Have Parasites*, for the O'Reilly Emerging Technology Conference, San Diego, CA, 16 March; also available online at http://craphound.com/complexecosystems.txt (accessed 4 April 2011).

Rivest, R., Shamir, A. and Adleman, L. (1978) 'A method for obtaining digital signatures and public-key cryptosystems', *Communications of the ACM*, vol. 21, no. 2, pp. 120–6.

Singh, S. (1999) *The Code Book*, London, Fourth Estate.

Tschabitscher, H. (2011) 'What Spam Is, Why It Is, and Why It is Bad' in *About.com* [online], http://email.about.com/od/spamandgettingridofit/a/what_is_spam.htm (accessed 11 July 2011).

Wikipedia (2011) 'Spam (electronic)' in *Wikipedia: the free encyclopedia* [online], http://en.wikipedia.org/wiki/Spam_(electronic) (accessed 4 April 2011).

Acknowledgements

Grateful acknowledgement is made to the following sources.

Text

Quotation p. 25: © 2011 Heinz Tschabitscher (http://email.about.com). Used with permission of About, Inc. which can be found online at www.about.com. All rights reserved

Figures

Figure 7: © McCullough, J. (2004) *Caution! Wireless Networking: Preventing a Data Disaster*, Wiley

Figure 25: © Taken from xkcd.com/792/. This file is licensed under the Creative Commons Attribution ShareAlike 2.0. http://creativecommons.org/licenses/by/2.0/deed.en

Digital rights, digital wrongs

Author: David Morse

Introduction

How to beat pirates and illegal downloaders

The BBC brought forward the transmission of series four [of award-winning US drama *Mad Men*] so it airs just after America rather than lagging by the usual six months. Why? In this age of instant technological gratification, it's the best way to satisfy devoted viewers and beat the pirates and illegal downloaders.

Preston, 2010, p. 3

This quotation, from an editorial in the *Radio Times*, raises a number of questions and issues that I will explore in this part of TU100. Who are the pirates, what are they pirating, how are they doing it and why? And in similar vein, what are people downloading illegally, why are they doing so and why is it illegal?

This block is concerned with the impact of ubiquitous computing on societies. In this part you are going to consider this idea from a largely commercial perspective involving the ownership, sale and protection of digital content. A vast range of people – from artists and actors to publishers and distributors – rely on their ability to generate an income from the replication and distribution of content: from novels and number one singles to the latest Hollywood blockbuster film. In the old analogue world of books and gramophone records, it was reasonably easy for people to control the replication and distribution of the content to which they had rights; hence they could protect their livelihoods. But in a digital world, where multiple perfect copies of original digital content can made and distributed around the world in milliseconds, things are very different.

I will be considering several issues stemming from this apparent ease of digital copying. Thus some of this part will be quite technical, while some of it will be more discursive.

The technical side relates to Part 3 of this block, where you studied cryptography and some of its applications. There you learned about the principles of encryption and found out how encryption underlies the secure exchange of data on the internet. In this part you will study another routine application of encryption, namely digital rights management (DRM). Briefly, DRM provides technical solutions to the problem of how to control access to digital content such as music, video or text. These solutions may prevent a user from copying material onto a disc or their computer, block conversion of that material from one format to another, or force the user to pay each time they access the material.

As you will see, DRM is only one way to manage access to digital content. The internet, businesses, laws and social norms all have a part to play too.

For this reason, DRM can be viewed as one element in a *socio-technical system* – that is, a system that involves the interaction of both people and technology in ways that are difficult or inappropriate to separate. Consideration of these interactions leads to the more discursive elements of this part, which continue the discussions around intellectual property law that you met in Block 3 Part 5.

In more detail, in this part I will:

1   examine some aspects of DRM technologies

2   review and extend some of the ideas involved in intellectual property law, particularly copyright and how it affects digital content

3   look at the recent history of how digital content has been sold and increasingly, now, is given away for nothing

4   give you some useful models of business and behaviour that will help you to think about some of the issues that are involved in this complex and rapidly evolving field.

Limitations of this part

It is worth outlining the boundaries that lack of space imposes on this part. I have not been able to write a wide-ranging discussion of what has happened or could happen to the whole panoply of content that is now available on the internet. That would be a whole module all by itself. Therefore, this part will not provide an all-encompassing discussion of the whole spectrum of broadcast, journalistic, audio and video content that is (or could be) made available over the internet. Nor will it discuss or make pronouncements on the array of business models that are now being employed to make money (or not) from publishing digital content on the internet. My coverage will necessarily be selective.

The copyright debate

Towards the end of this part I will ask you to listen to an audio debate between three people who are well known for their views on digital content and its production, consumption and protection. While you are listening to the debate, I will ask you to use your SenseBoard to record your reactions to the debate as it takes place and then compare your opinions to those of your fellow students on TU100.

> Note that this debate is the main focus of Session 5, which is presented online. You should allow 2–3 hours for this online study.

By way of an introduction to some of the issues that will be discussed in the debate and in the rest of this part, I have produced a short audio introduction that highlights some of these issues.

Activity 1 (exploratory)

Listen to the introduction to copyright and the short discussion that follows, which you will find in the resources page associated with this part on the TU100 website. As you do so, I recommend that you make some brief notes to help you listen actively and concentrate on what is being said. You may find it necessary to rewind each audio and listen to it again to help you in your note-taking.

Learning outcomes

Your study of this part will help you to do the following.

Knowledge and understanding

- Describe the main components and operations of a typical digital rights management (DRM) system such as the DVD content scrambling system.

- Describe some of the vulnerabilities to attack of digital rights management systems and the ways in which some DRM systems have been circumvented (e.g. the 'analogue hole').

- Summarise the different forms of legal protection that may be used to protect intellectual property (copyright, patents, trademarks and design rights).

- Understand some of the incentives in freely giving away digital content.

- Demonstrate an awareness of the different stakeholders involved in the digital supply chain and their different perspectives on copyright and digital rights management.

- Demonstrate an awareness of the legal, business and ethical contexts for the distribution of digital works.

- Understand the constraints that affect behaviour according to Lessig (law, social norms, market forces and architecture) and how they interact, reinforcing or undermining each other.

Cognitive skills

- Analyse the legitimacy of consumption of copyrighted material, both analogue (e.g. paper) and digital (e.g. film).

- Analyse a given business model from the perspectives of the three stakeholders (creative, commercial and consumer) in the digital supply chain.

- Identify the constraints (according to Lessig) on behaviour with respect to the consumption of digital content.

Digital rights management (DRM)

1

The ease with which digital content – in whatever format – can be copied has led individuals and businesses engaged in publishing and distributing digital content to seek mechanisms to retain control over how their material is accessed and used, to protect their revenue. DRM attempts to provide technological mechanisms for control. In this session I will describe the principles of two DRM technologies: one for films and one for music.

1.1 What is DRM?

Digital rights management (DRM) is a collection of technologies aimed at controlling digital content. Using DRM, a distributor or manufacturer can stipulate just how their product is to be used: the type of equipment it is compatible with, whether it can be copied or altered, even who can use the product. The advent of DRM heralded a fundamental change in the way consumers use goods and services.

Traditionally, a producer's relationship with a consumer ends when the user purchases the product. For instance, when you buy a book you may simply read it, but alternatively you can mark pages with notes, tear out pages, give the book to a friend or even burn it. Similarly, when you buy a CD you consider it to be yours to do with as you wish (subject to copyright law). Whether you play the music, turn the contents into MP3 files or even use the disc as a coaster, the producer has no direct control over how you use or misuse the product.

However, this is not the case with content that is protected by DRM, such as films. Here, the long arm of the producer extends to actually preventing consumers from using the content in certain ways – copying it, for example – after the product has been purchased.

1.2 DRM and film

The *content scrambling system (CSS)* was introduced in 1996 to protect pre-recorded commercially produced DVDs from unauthorised copying. You don't need to know the precise details of how it works; the following is just an outline.

I have not included the additional complications of regional codes and sector keys, which can be used in the encryption/decryption processes but do not affect the basic principles involved.

The system is based on encryption involving different kinds of keys. Each DVD manufacturer embeds into their DVD players a fixed number of *player keys* that can be used to play any DVD. A total of 409 player keys are available, but only a subset of these keys is included in DVD players made by any one manufacturer. Each player key is a secret key that is part of the same encryption scheme.

Each DVD has a table stored in a hidden area that holds encrypted versions of the *disc key* used by that particular disc. Entry 1 in this table holds the value of the disc key encrypted with player key 1, entry 2 holds the value of the disc key encrypted with player key 2, and so on until entry 409 holds the value of the disc key encrypted with player key 409. In addition, each disc stores another version of the disc key, this time encrypted with the disc key itself (the encrypted version is called the *disc key hash*).

Should an attacker get to know any of the 409 player keys then that key is revoked (i.e. removed from the table on all new DVDs).

When requested to play a disc, the DVD player will select one of its player keys and use this key to decrypt the corresponding entry in the table of encrypted disc keys on the DVD (Figure 1a). This should result in the disc key. To check that the DVD player has correctly decrypted the disc key and can thus decrypt the DVD, it will use this disc key to decrypt the disc key hash (Figure 1b). If the result of this decryption is the value of the disc key then the DVD player has correctly obtained the disc key; if the values do not match then the DVD player tries another of its player keys. This step is used to verify that the disc key has been decrypted correctly, in case the encrypted version was read incorrectly from the disc.

Each disc also contains an encrypted version of the *title key* for each work stored on the disc. The title key is encrypted using the disc key and hence can be decrypted once the disc key has been found by the DVD player (Figure 1c). Once the title key has been found, it can be used to decrypt the actual content of the disc (Figure 1d).

Standard disc copying does not copy a disc's table of disc keys, and that makes such copies unplayable: if a CSS-compatible DVD player tries to play a disc without a table, it cannot calculate the disc key and so will not play the disc (Figure 2).

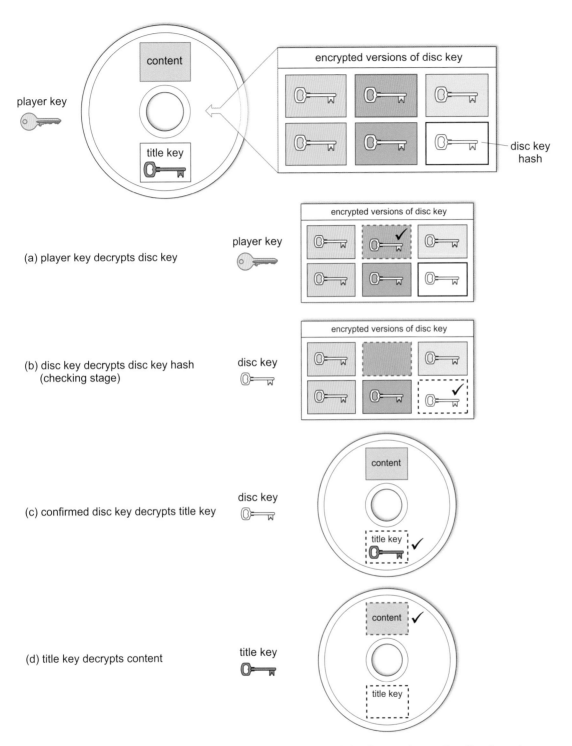

Figure 1 The content scrambling system: the top part of the figure shows the disc keys in a separate hidden area on the DVD and the title key for an item (e.g. a film) on the DVD, while steps (a)–(d) underneath show the process a DVD player must go through in order to play the content

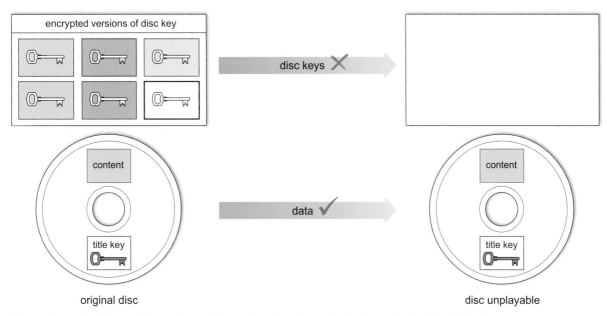

Figure 2   Copying a CSS-protected disc: the data is copied but not the table of disc keys

Activity 2 (self-assessment)

Why is more than one player key used in the CSS scheme?

DeCSS

There is a perception that it is only a matter of time before any DRM system is hacked. In fact, the content scrambling system was compromised in 1999 when the Norwegian programmer Jon Lech Johansen released the computer program DeCSS, which is capable of decrypting CSS content. Johansen was subsequently taken to court by the Norwegian economic crime unit Økokrim, following a complaint by the US DVD Copy Control Association and the Motion Picture Association. Johansen denied writing the decryption code in DeCSS and argued that he had not obtained any illegal information since he owned the DVDs that he had decrypted – according to Norwegian law it is legal to make copies for personal use. Johansen was acquitted of all charges in 2003.

1.3   DRM and music

Beginning in the late 1990s, the *Secure Digital Music Initiative (SDMI)* was an attempt to secure all parts of the music market, including the hardware for playing and recording music and the recordings themselves. It was led by the SDMI Consortium, an industry body comprising all the major electronics manufacturers, record publishers and software companies.

Aims of SDMI

The intention of the SDMI Consortium was to prevent hardware and software music players from duplicating digital content. It was viewed as important that any new system should be capable of incorporating old players and recordings, since it was unacceptable to render people's existing music libraries obsolete. In addition, though it would have been easier to develop a completely new hardware and software format, companies already had considerable investment in the CD manufacturing process and recognised that it would take a long time for a new music format to become established in the marketplace. Hence SDMI aimed to retain the existing CD format.

The system developed by SDMI was based on protecting recorded music using a series of *digital watermarks* that would be recognised by SDMI-compliant machines. Existing CD player formats would gradually be upgraded to become SDMI-compliant, recognising the watermarks as I will now describe.

Digital watermarks

A watermark is often used to establish the authenticity of paper documents. A mark is impressed into the paper during the manufacturing process and cannot be altered or removed without damaging the document. Bank notes often use a watermark that is only revealed when they are held up to the light.

A digital watermark is a stream of bits that is added during the creation of a file to the bits in that file that carry the information. Ideally the watermark is undetectable during normal use, but it can be retrieved using specialised software.

SDMI used two watermarks in every file. The first was known as the *robust watermark*. This watermark would survive compression, decompression, changes in file format and copying between devices – even if the machines were not themselves SDMI-compliant. The robust watermark indicated that a file was SDMI-compatible and therefore not intended for copying. When an SDMI file was played in a SDMI-compliant player, the player would look for the robust watermark. If it found one it would look for a second watermark – the *fragile watermark*. This watermark would not survive the process of being copied, compressed or altered. In other words, any copies made from an SDMI master would lack the fragile watermark but retain the robust watermark, indicating that the music was protected under SDMI. An SDMI-compliant player presented with an SDMI file without a fragile watermark should refuse to play the music.

The watermarks were placed in the audible component of the data (as opposed to other data such as the audio track index) to ensure that the robust watermark would be copied, even if the copy was made using a

non-SDMI machine. The fragile watermark would be lost in the copying process, preventing the pirate copies from being played on SDMI machines.

Since the watermarks were placed in the audible component of the data, they made changes to it, which meant that an SDMI recording was not a completely faithful reproduction of the original music. However, SDMI proponents were confident that these changes were so small that they were undetectable, and in fact were far smaller than the distortions induced by faults in the physical structure of the disc or by imperfections in the listener's audio system.

Activity 3 (self-assessment)

(a) If an SDMI-compatible CD were copied, would the copy have the robust watermark? Would it have the fragile watermark?

(b) Explain whether an old, non-SDMI-compliant player would play a pirated CD.

The expectation was that the music industry would rely on the continual replacement of older machines with newer SDMI-compliant hardware, gradually eliminating the pirate market. It is interesting to examine a little more closely the strategy for introducing SDMI.

Creating an SDMI world

The SDMI Consortium constructed a strategy for introducing the technology in two phases. Phase 1 was to introduce SDMI players and music into the commercial market, and was aimed at getting people to buy SDMI recordings. During this time, the vast majority of players would not be SDMI-compliant and the user would not notice any change to the way they used music.

With time, as SDMI became more common, the industry would introduce phase 2 of SDMI. Phase 2 was intended to tempt users into buying SDMI-compliant equipment by issuing CDs with special features such as bonus tracks, interviews and discounts against further purchases. There were also plans to issue music over the internet on a pay-per-listen basis.

When a CD with bonus content was placed into an SDMI-compliant player, the player would read some specially inserted data and inform the user that phase 2 SDMI was available. If the user chose to upgrade, they would download the phase 2 software required to make their player fully SDMI-enabled either from the disc or over the internet. If they chose not to upgrade to phase 2 SDMI, they could continue to use their existing collection of music as before, but would be unable to access any of the phase 2 extras. Naturally, any players issued after the beginning of phase 2 would have had the features enabled by default.

SDMI – was the system fatally flawed?

SDMI would stand or fall on the strength of its watermark system. And it contained a weakness: the requirement for compatibility with older players and music recordings. To ensure this compatibility, if an SDMI player found no watermark on a recording, it proceeded on the basis that the music was recorded before the advent of SDMI and was not protected. (The alternative strategy, that an SDMI player would not play a piece of music without a watermark, would have made people's music collections obsolete overnight.) Therefore, any file without recognisable SDMI watermarks would not be considered to be an SDMI file.

In turn, this meant that if the watermarks could be removed from an SDMI file, or the watermarks were altered sufficiently to lose their identity, then the recording would no longer be treated by an SDMI player as an SDMI recording and the player would simply play the recording. Removing the watermark was thus a potential way in which SDMI recordings could be pirated. However, the SDMI Consortium were so confident in their watermarking system that in September 2000 they issued a challenge known as *HackSDMI* to the computing community.

The HackSDMI Challenge

The HackSDMI Challenge was actually split into six sub-challenges (A to F), four of which were concerned with watermarking. Since the HackSDMI Challenge was extremely technical, here I will discuss only the first sub-challenge – known as *Sub-challenge A.*

Entrants to the HackSDMI Challenge were given three pieces of music:

- *song 1* – a piece of music without any SDMI watermarks
- *song 2* – the same as song 1, but with the SDMI watermarks
- *song 3* – a different piece of music also containing the SDMI watermarks.

Sub-challenge A was to either remove the watermarks from song 3 entirely or render them useless so that the song would lose its SDMI protection.

The 'simplest' attacks on SDMI attempted to isolate the watermarks. Songs 1 and 2 differed only in that song 2 contained the watermark. The general procedure that entrants to the challenge followed was to sample the songs, then for each sample interval compare the information in song 2 with that in song 1. Any difference had to be due to the SDMI watermark. 'Subtracting' the difference from song 2 removed the watermark. Since the researchers then had the SDMI watermark (the difference between song 1 and song 2), they were able to 'subtract' that information from song 3 to produce an unprotected version of the music (Figure 3). This might sound rather simple, but in fact it was a highly complex business; hence the SDMI Consortium's confidence in their system.

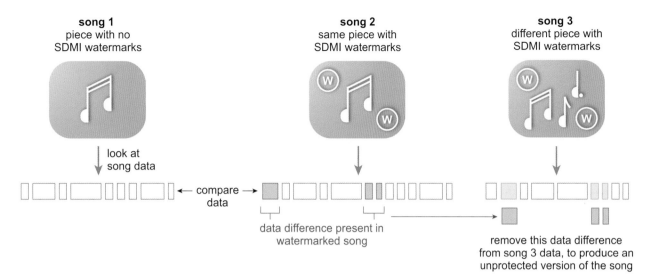

song 1
piece with no
SDMI watermarks

song 2
same piece with
SDMI watermarks

song 3
different piece with
SDMI watermarks

look at
song data

← compare →
data

data difference present in
watermarked song

remove this data difference
from song 3 data, to produce an
unprotected version of the song

Figure 3   Solving the first part of the HackSDMI Challenge

The results of HackSDMI

In October 2000 the online magazine *Salon* reported that SDMI had been comprehensively defeated. At first the story was denied by the SDMI Consortium, but by the end of October it was clear that SDMI was in serious trouble. A team from Princeton University publicly claimed to have broken SDMI using a variety of techniques. They had made an attempt on all six sub-challenges and were satisfied that they had succeeded in all of them. The HackSDMI Challenge appeared to have backfired on the SDMI Consortium.

However, the HackSDMI Challenge had a sting in its tail. Participants in the challenge had to sign non-disclosure agreements with the SDMI Consortium, preventing them from publishing their work. (This had incensed many researchers, who publicly called for non-cooperation.) So the Princeton team announced that they would present their work at a computer security conference. The team's lawyers then warned that they might be vulnerable to prosecution under the US Digital Millennium Copyright Act (DMCA), which forbids circumvention of copy-protection systems. While the HackSDMI Challenge could be seen as research, publication of the work would allow anyone to copy the Princeton techniques and defeat SDMI. This warning was reinforced by the threat of a lawsuit from the SDMI Consortium and the Recording Industry Association of America (RIAA) should the team publish. The Princeton team withdrew the paper from the conference.

The team then turned to a judge, asking for protection from prosecution should they publish their work. This was almost unheard of in the USA. The case attracted enormous public attention and the support of the Electronic Frontier Foundation (see Box 1). Eventually, the SDMI Consortium relented; by August 2001, the RIAA said it had no objection

to the work being published. The Princeton team presented their work to another computing conference and their paper was published on the Web.

> ### Box 1 The Electronic Frontier Foundation (EFF)
>
> The EFF is an organisation committed to educating the public and legislators on technological issues. It is concerned with the effects of new technology on people's rights and has campaigned on issues such as cryptography, telephone-tapping, censorship and copyright. Although the EFF is largely concerned with developments in the USA, its campaigning stance has been copied by other organisations around the world.

The end of SDMI?

As if the results of the HackSDMI Challenge weren't devastating enough, internal bickering ensured that the SDMI Consortium quickly fell apart. Officially SDMI has been on hold since May 2001, although few people expect it ever to see the light of day. Nowadays, any CD that follows the standard for CDs and thus is able to bear the trademark *Compact Disc Digital Audio* logo will not have any form of DRM. However, some non-standard types of CD have been developed that have some form of copy protection – for example, the Extended Copy Protection (XMG) implemented by Sony BMG in 2005.

The legal action against the Princeton University team that was threatened by the RIAA has had at least one unintended and unanticipated long-term consequence, namely that academic research into DRM and related copy-protection technologies in the USA has declined to virtually nil. In an article on his *Copyright and Technology* blog, Bill Rosenblatt – a consultant to the content industries – described a search that he had carried out in the IEEE Xplore digital library for papers published that related to digital rights research. Between 2008 and mid-2010 (when he carried out his investigation), 40% of the papers originated from China, 27% were from the rest of Asia, 20% were from Europe and less than 4% were from the USA (Rosenblatt, 2010a).

1.4   DRM: keeping honest people honest?

So what is the point of DRM? Many people have asked this question, ever since early DRM systems were cracked. At least one industry source casts digital rights management as the friend of the consumer, keeping us on the right side of the law:

> Content owners use DRMs because it provides casual, honest users with guidelines for using and consuming content based on the usage

rights that were acquired. Without the use of DRMs, honest consumers would have no guidelines and might eventually come to totally disregard copyright and therefore become a pirate, resulting in great harm to content creators.

Dan Glickman, Motion Picture Association of America, quoted in BBC (2006)

The sentiment behind this quotation riles many activists and consumer groups because of its suggestion that we are all of a piratical persuasion and that DRM is the only thing keeping honest people honest. Many activists also object to the use of the term 'pirate' for those people who disregard copyright when using digital content, arguing that this is a strongly emotive word for a casual act that is often a consequence of poor knowledge or understanding of the law (see Box 2).

Box 2 Illegal music downloads

In a survey of more than 5000 people carried out in the UK in September 2010, 28.8% of Britons aged between 16 and 54 (that's around 7.7 million people) admitted that they had unlawfully downloaded or shared music. The report by Harris Interactive also estimated that nearly three-quarters of the music tracks downloaded in 2010 were acquired illegally, amounting to 1.2 billion tracks (BPI, 2010). This exceeds the total number of individual tracks that have ever been downloaded legally in the UK (up to 2010), which the BPI (the British Recorded Music Industry) estimates to be about 1 billion.

Against DRM

In addition to average users, for whom almost any type of security measure will work, there is a second group of users on the internet – namely hackers.

To the hackers, DRM has yet to prove itself invulnerable. One reason why it is so difficult to stop determined hackers breaking schemes that use encryption to protect content is that the content must be decrypted in order for people to be able to view it. If the decryption process runs on a PC, experienced hackers can extract the unencrypted content so that it can be copied. This has been called the 'logical fallacy' of DRM: that the very people whom we want to prevent from having access to the decryption keys (hackers) must be able to view content protected by DRM in order to be able to view content that they have obtained legally.

The existence of the *analogue hole* is another reason why many people argue that DRM systems are fundamentally flawed and will never work. The analogue hole has always existed, but has only become an issue of

importance since the invention and widespread deployment of DRM technologies. The term derives from the fact that our senses – through which we perceive the world – are analogue, not digital. Therefore, digital content from any form of audio or video must be converted into an analogue signal before the viewer can see or hear it. No DRM system yet invented is capable of controlling content in this form. Consequently, it is possible to circumvent DRM systems (for fair use or other reasons) by intercepting and copying the analogue audio and video signals, or even using a video camera to record the screen displaying the images and sound that you want to copy.

Activity 4 (self-assessment)

Why is the quality of a recording copied from an analogue signal as described above likely to be inferior to the original?

Finally, there is an argument that DRM is doomed to failure because it is rooted in antiquated business models in which middlemen such as publishers make money from the replication and distribution of content. This argument is based on the premise that with the ease of digital content copying on the internet, giving content away free is the only workable model. I will take up this point later in this part.

1.5   Conclusion

In this session you have studied the principles of two digital rights management technologies that have been applied to film and music: CSS and SDMI. I examined the weaknesses of both systems and described how they have been hacked. I rounded off the session by describing some perceptions of and attitudes towards DRM.

This session should have helped you with the following learning outcomes.

- Describe the main components and operations of a typical digital rights management (DRM) system such as the DVD content scrambling system.
- Describe some of the vulnerabilities to attack of digital rights management systems and the ways in which some DRM systems have been circumvented (e.g. the 'analogue hole').

2 Owning and controlling information

You have learned that DRM offers technical mechanisms for protecting information from unauthorised use. That is, DRM contributes to the enforcement of intellectual property laws such as copyright laws. I will start off this session by reviewing and extending some ideas about intellectual property laws that you learned about in Block 3 Part 5, before discussing copyright law in a little more detail.

In the previous session you discovered that DRM systems are not infallible. I also noted, right at the end of the session, that the very concept upon which DRM is based – protecting digital content – is being challenged by some people. This leads me to the wider question of who owns information in general. With the internet enabling the increasing accessibility of information, does it even make sense to talk about owning information? In this session I will also consider questions of this kind.

2.1 Intellectual property law

The digital revolution has made the tasks of writing text, composing music, creating images and producing films easier than ever. These can then be advertised or distributed via the Web. (For example, online photo libraries allow purchasers to browse through a gallery of photographs and download them upon payment; to prevent people from simply copying the photos using, say, screen capture techniques, the images in the gallery are sometimes published with a large 'watermark' on them that would identify them as being obtained illegally.) With the advent of the personal computer, small companies specialising in media production have flourished. It is possible for a relative novice to create, edit and distribute a film or musical composition using a single computer.

The flip side of the coin is that the digital revolution has also made it easy to duplicate and steal such materials. In Block 3 Part 5 you learned about the legal protections given to information and ideas. The overall field of the law that deals with intangible property that is the result of creativity is known as *intellectual property rights (IPR)*. Intellectual property rights within this area of law in the UK are granted by the *Intellectual Property Office (IPO)*, an official government body.

A link to the IPO website is given in the online resources page associated with this part.

I will provide a brief overview of what you learned in Block 3 Part 5 before studying some aspects of copyright law in more detail.

Activity 5 (self-assessment)

(a) In Block 3 Part 5 you learned about three broad areas of intellectual property law: patents, trademarks and copyright. Briefly summarise each of these concepts.

(b) What is meant by a licence in the context of copyright?

Design rights

There is one other significant area of intellectual property law: that of *design rights*, which apply to the physical appearance of an item or part of an item. The appearance of the object is not concerned with how that item works or what it does; instead, it concentrates on what the item looks like. Features such as the shape, texture, colour and material used in the item are important to the design and can be protected through design rights. The purpose of design rights protection is to prevent others from copying your design. You might imagine the fashion industry to hold many design rights, but in fact that is far from the case (see Box 3). Designs protected by design rights include children's toys and domestic furniture.

Like other forms of intellectual property protection, design rights have to be registered. Once registered, they must also be renewed – every five years for up to 25 years after initial registration of the design.

Box 3 Intellectual property in the fashion industry

It may surprise you to learn that the fashion industry has very little intellectual property protection. The fashion industry does not enjoy the protection of patents, copyright or even design rights; its principal form of intellectual property protection is trademarks. This is one reason why trademarks are fiercely protected in the fashion industry and why so many items of fashion have trademarks that are on the outside and designed to be seen. While a third party can copy the design of a dress, they cannot copy the designer label too because being a trademark, that is protected.

Why doesn't the fashion industry have copyright or design rights protection? Because the courts have consistently argued that clothing is a type of 'useful article'. Thus the cut of the cloth, the position of the seams and the design of the garment as a whole are not protected since these are utilitarian articles. Even costumes that may well not be practical or in any sense utilitarian are not protected by copyright.

Therefore, the fashion industry exists in a culture of copying without having to ask permission or worry about being sued for copyright infringement. It is this lack of protection that is one of the reasons why the fashion industry is so creative, vibrant and fast-moving. Imagine how much more slowly fashion trends would move if fashion houses had to ask permission of each other every time they wanted to copy part of a garment from another designer. (Though note that a designer can own the copyright in a drawing of the garment, just not copyright in the garment itself.)

So how does the fashion industry, and particularly the luxury end of the industry, survive in a culture of rampant copying? Essentially, it survives through market segmentation (dividing the market for clothes into homogeneous groups of consumers who differentiate themselves on price amongst other criteria) and the protection offered by trademarks. As Tom Ford (a designer who used to work for Gucci) put it, 'the counterfeit customer is not the Gucci customer'.

2.2   Intellectual property protection in different industries

In Section 2.1 I indicated that there are some industries, such as the fashion industry, that do not enjoy the same intellectual property protection as other industries. Are there other examples of industries that are in the same position as the fashion industry? It turns out that there are. Typically, those industries that deal with utilitarian articles such as cars or furniture are not protected by copyright because you cannot copyright the overall design of the product (although design rights can be applied to the overall appearance of an article). As you saw in the case of the fashion industry, such items are regarded by the courts as too 'utilitarian'. Likewise with food – you cannot protect the look and feel of even the most unique or unusual dish. Neither can you copyright a recipe, because it is a set of instructions – which is not copyrightable.

In contrast, some industries (such as the media industries) have a great deal of intellectual property protection because of the nature of their products – intellectual property. Figure 4 shows how these two different groups of industries – those that are given low levels of protection by intellectual property laws and those operating in areas that enjoy high levels of protection – compare in terms of their gross sales of goods.

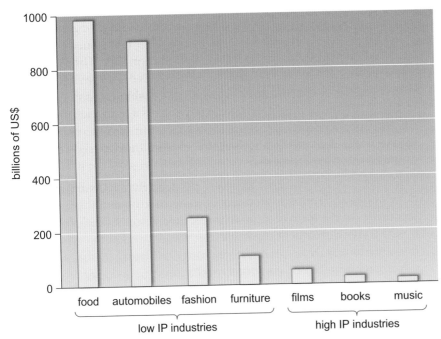

Figure 4   **Gross sales of goods in the USA in 2007, in billions of US dollars**

Activity 6 (self-assessment)

You might expect high levels of intellectual property protection to correlate with large industries where intellectual property protection is necessary to protect revenues and activities. Does Figure 4 support this expectation?

2.3 Copyright law

Unlike patents and trademarks, copyright is an automatic right given to the creator of any suitable material – it is not granted by an outside body. The copyright symbol, ©, is used to denote that a work is copyrighted, but its use is not mandatory, so just because a work doesn't have a copyright symbol doesn't mean that the work is not protected by copyright. This is important to note when it comes to using copyrighted works. However, before considering our rights when it comes to using and reusing copyrighted works, it is instructive to look briefly at the history of copyright.

As you saw in Block 3 Part 5, copyright was designed to benefit all parts of society – the creator would be rewarded for their work by being able to charge for copies in the knowledge that no one else could do likewise,

whilst the rest of society would benefit by having access to the work when the copyright period expired.

Three main points of relevance to this part are set out by Corrigan and Rogers (2005, pp. 154–6) in their paper on the economics of copyright:

1   Copyright law is continuously evolving and developing as technical advances pose new threats to people's livelihoods, from the stationers and printers of the 1500s to the film producers of the twentieth century, and beyond to the digital media producers of the twenty-first century.

2   The types of work that are subject to copyright are expanding too. First, books and other printed works were copyrighted; then, as sound recording (in the form of gramophones, then cassette tapes, followed by CDs) was developed, copyright law was expanded to encompass these media too. Now we have broadcast and digital media, all of which are protected by copyright legislation.

3   Over the course of history, the term of copyright has gradually extended and shows no sign of becoming any shorter. For example, in the UK, the Statute of Anne in 1710 is thought to be the first copyright law, under which the copyright term was 14 years. In 1908, the Berne Convention (to which the UK is a signatory) recommended a minimum term of copyright of the life of the author plus 50 years. Finally, in 1993, the EU harmonised copyright legislation in its member states to specify a term of the life of the author plus 70 years.

The Digital Economy Act 2010

The Digital Economy Act 2010 was rushed into UK law during the final days of the Labour government that was in power between 1997 and 2010. The Act implements aspects of government policy on digital media that were set out in the *Digital Britain* government report published in June 2009.

Activity 7 (exploratory)

You learned a little about the *Digital Britain* report in Part 1 of this block. Can you recall any of the themes of the government of the time's vision for a digital Britain?

Comment

Block 5 Part 1 alluded to three themes:

1   modernising UK government by improving the way in which it uses and manages digital information

2   improving the digital communications infrastructure in the UK

3   enabling everyone to participate in a digital society.

The Digital Economy Act 2010 attempts to implement measures in each of the areas mentioned in the previous activity, but in addition it attempts to develop a strong legal framework within which creative industries can be protected in a digital world. It is this theme of the Digital Economy Act that is most relevant to this part, and in fact this is seen as the most controversial part of the Act. It sets out a procedure for dealing with online copyright infringement by individuals that has become known colloquially as the 'three strikes' system, or officially as a 'graduated response'.

The way it works is as follows. Copyright owners identify instances of copyright infringement. They then report these instances to the suspect's internet service provider (ISP). The ISP will review the evidence provided by the copyright owner and, if appropriate, send a warning letter to the suspect. The ISP has to keep a record of how many times it has had to write to each subscriber; if this reaches a certain threshold (currently set at three times in a year – hence the *three* in 'three strikes') then the ISP can be asked to hand over the names of the offenders to copyright owners. Penalties such as limiting the subscriber's use of the internet by measures such as bandwidth capping or even cutting off access to the internet have been proposed, but these will require the intervention of the Secretary of State according to the draft code of practice issued by Ofcom and due to come into force in late 2011.

Permitted use of copyright works

As it has developed, the copyright system has had to balance the rights given to creators to create new things that are protected under copyright law against the reduction in public access to created works that copyright protection affords. This is not easy, and many would argue that as copyright law has become all-encompassing and lasts for longer and longer periods, the balance is shifting away from those who want access to copyrighted works and towards those who create or make money from copyrighted works. I will discuss this balancing act in more detail shortly.

You may well be aware that there are certain exceptions to copyright legislation that allow limited copying. Typically, these come under the heading of 'fair use' and allow you to make single copies of a copyrighted work for the purposes of non-commercial research or private study. An example of fair use is that you are permitted to include small parts of copyrighted work in your answers to assignment questions set in this module, as long as you acknowledge where you have taken them from. Another example in a different context is that you are allowed to record a television programme in order to watch it at a time of your choice (known as *time-shifting*).

The OU Library website has guidelines on how to interpret this aspect of fair use in the context of your own study. Information about how to credit the sources of copyrighted materials can be found on the TU100 website.

Breaching copyright

Copyright laws make breaches of copyright illegal, and hence the person who broke the law becomes liable to legal action. However, bringing legal

action against someone who has broken copyright law may not be feasible, perhaps because of the costs involved or the number of people who have broken the law in that particular way. For example, you saw in Box 2 that an estimated 7.7 million people in the UK have unlawfully downloaded or shared music. Even if that figure is an overestimate, the chances of being caught – let alone prosecuted – are very low. This argument may tempt some people to download or share digital content illegally – if they are even aware that their actions are illegal in the first place.

Having said that, copyright owners do take action against illegal file sharing. For example, in the summer of 2010, solicitors acting for the dance music label Ministry of Sound sent letters to 2000 individuals who they claimed had infringed Ministry of Sound's copyright after downloading and sharing music. This case is somewhat controversial, having been brought by a firm (ACS:Law) that has been criticised by the BPI (British Phonographic Industry, the trade body that represents the recording industry) for its approach to dealing with illegal file sharing. Indeed, the BPI holds the position that legal action should be used as a last resort against persistent or serious offenders.

Analogue copying

In the past, other factors such as the quality of the copies that can be made or the cost of making copies may have deterred you from copying copyrighted works illicitly. Such factors are far less significant with digital works.

Suppose, for example, that someone lends you some pre-recorded music or you borrow an album from a library. The same copyright laws make copying the album illegal, but the quality of the copy and the economics of making the copy have changed. In the past, when recordings were made for playing on gramophones, few people had the equipment needed to make copies of gramophone records, so it didn't happen very much. With the advent of the cassette tape, it was possible to copy recordings from one cassette tape to another using a dual-cassette tape machine, and illegal copying of music became a much greater problem than it had been. However, the copy was, of necessity, a poorer copy of the recording than the original. Both gramophones and cassettes are analogue recording technologies, so any copy of the recording was bound to be an imperfect copy of the original because of imperfections in the reproduction process. The same is true of video-cassette tape. This is another analogue recording medium so the reproduction will be imperfect.

Activity 8 (exploratory)

Suppose someone lends you a book or you borrow one from the library. Copying the whole book is illegal under copyright law, and that in itself would deter most people from taking a copy. But even setting aside issues

of copyright, people generally don't photocopy whole books – they tend to buy their own copy of the book rather than photocopy someone else's illegally. For the majority of people, most of the time, making illegal copies of books just isn't worthwhile.

List some problems that are inherent in photocopying books that deter people from doing this.

Comment

I thought of the following.

- Copying a whole book using a photocopier is tedious.
- The copy may cost you almost as much as buying a copy of the book.
- The illegal photocopy will probably be a poorer copy than the original, perhaps on inconveniently sized paper, in loose-leaf format.

Digital copying

With the advent of the CD and then the DVD, it became possible to make perfect copies of an original recording because these are digital formats, so any copies made will be perfect copies of the original. (Though note that if the copy is stored in a format that is less good than the original (e.g. MP3), such as might occur when you 'rip' a CD, then the copy may not be as good as the original.)

Programs are available that copy the contents of a CD and store it on a computer. This process is called 'ripping'.

With a personal computer you can (digital rights management and copyright law apart) make copies of the original almost instantly and at very little cost. Now that many people have broadband and are connected to the internet, it is very easy to send copies of the recording to people by email, or place the file on a peer-to-peer network and let anyone on the internet have access to it.

In fact several authors, including Cory Doctorow and Kevin Kelly, have argued that the internet is a giant copying machine:

> Computers are machines for copying data. A good computer is one that copies well, quickly and cheaply. The internet is a machine for moving copies of data around. When the internet works well, it copies data quickly and cheaply.

> Doctorow, 2007

Copying is an essential aspect of the internet, even though we may not always be aware of it. If you send me a file by email, you send me a copy of that file. Copies of the file and the email will be held on various servers on the internet as the email is transmitted from you to me. If you place the file on a server so that I can download it, unless that was your only copy of the file and I delete the file from the server when I download it then you have given me a copy of the file – you haven't lent it to me.

2.4 Piracy

When you buy music on CD or a film on DVD, what exactly do you own? The answer is more complicated than you might think. You own the case, the printed slip and the physical disc itself, but you do not own the information stored on the disc (the music or film). The information remains under the copyright of the copyright holder – usually either the artist or the studio that published the work. When you buy the disc you are granted a licence to *play* the material. You are not (in the UK at least) permitted to copy, redistribute or edit the information in any way.

Piracy is the illegal duplication of materials that are protected by intellectual property law; it is part of a global counterfeiting industry that costs the creative industries many billions of pounds every year. Traditionally counterfeiting has been concerned with attempting to copy currencies or luxury goods, but forgers are increasingly making fakes of other valuable products such as computer memory, life-saving pharmaceuticals and even aircraft components.

One of the most serious piracy problems is the duplication of digital content – music, films and computer software. This has been a thriving industry for many years; as previously described, audio piracy became a problem with the arrival of the cheap cassette recorder in the 1960s, and piracy of films became significant with the development of cheap video recorders. However, piracy was always limited by three major factors, the first two of which I alluded to in the previous section.

1   It was time-consuming to make a copy. Few people could duplicate more than one copy at a time and those copies would take a considerable amount of time to make.

2   Copies were invariably inferior to the original. Most people would continue to purchase the original item knowing that they would get a faithful reproduction.

3   Gaining access to pirated materials was difficult for people without contacts in the film or music industry, or required them to deal with people on the fringes of criminal culture.

Computer technology has transformed the potential for piracy; at a stroke it has removed the limitations inherent in previous technologies. A computer can make a thousand copies of a piece of digital information in little more time than it takes to make a single copy, and every copy will be an exact duplicate of the original. The internet also provides the perfect distribution method for pirated information. People connect to a website or a file server and download copies directly to their hard disks. There is no need to find a dealer in pirated material; a search engine can do the job.

One of the few remaining restraints on piracy is the sheer size of media files. However, even this restraint can be overcome with digital

technology; two data formats, MP3 and DivX, allow digital copies – of poorer quality – of a very small size to be made, and these can be transferred quickly over the internet. Now, almost anyone can receive digital music over their phone line; with broadband, receiving digital copies of films is possible.

In Block 4 Part 1 you learned about the music-sharing system Napster, which was created in order to make it easier to share music encoded in MP3 format on the internet. You learned that Napster was vulnerable to legal action because it held information about its users' music on its central servers. More recent file-swapping systems have dispensed with the need for these servers and are known as *peer-to-peer client programs*. Peer-to-peer systems are less vulnerable to legal action because of the lack of centralised control, but that doesn't make their activities any more legal (see Box 4). Of course, the problem is not the file-sharing networks themselves but the nature of the files that are often shared over such networks. It is perfectly possible for these networks to be entirely legal, for example sharing files that the users have created themselves.

Box 4 LimeWire

LimeWire was a free, peer-to-peer file-sharing program that ran on operating systems that supported the Java software platform. In October 2010, a US federal judge found the LimeWire company guilty of assisting users to commit copyright infringement and thus granted the music industry's request to shut down the file-sharing service based on this program. This also affected the LimeWire Store that used the same program to sell and distribute music online, entirely legitimately. This service was shut down in December 2010.

2.5   Information wants to be free

Piracy of digital content shows no sign of diminishing. DRM systems are hacked, copyright is infringed and prosecuting the perpetrators is complex and costly, or proves impossible. What can society do in the face of such a problem? Some people suggest that a radical rethink of the notion of owning and controlling digital content is required.

In 2009 the Editor in Chief of *Wired* magazine, Chris Anderson, published a book entitled *Free: The Future of a Radical Price* (Anderson, 2009). In this book, Anderson elaborates on a statement that most people attribute to Stewart Brand: 'Information wants to be free'.

Stewart Brand is a writer, critical thinker and co-founder of the Long Now Foundation.

On the one hand information wants to be expensive, because it's so valuable. The right information in the right place just changes your life. On the other hand, information wants to be free, because the cost of getting it out is getting lower and lower all the time. So you have these two fighting against each other.

Stewart Brand, speaking at the Hackers' Conference in 1984

Through a series of case studies and examples, Anderson demonstrates that in the internet age, there is a downward pressure on the price of information (more generally intellectual property – ideas rather than things) to the extent that information has no value. He asserts that creators of digital content should give away what they have created and somehow make money around what they have given away. As he says:

In the digital realm you can try to keep Free at bay with laws and locks, but eventually the force of economic gravity will win.

Anderson, 2009, p. 241

Activity 9 (self-assessment)

Based on what you have read so far in this part, what do you think might be meant by 'laws and locks'?

I will explore some of the ways in which money can be and has been made by giving content away later in this part, but before I do that, I want to explore the 'force of economic gravity' that Anderson refers to in the above quotation from his book.

The impetus to freedom

Anderson's argument is based on four claims. The first is that the cost of the digital technologies from which the internet is constructed is constantly falling (you will have met this concept before in earlier parts of TU100 when you studied Moore's Law). If you have recently bought yourself a new computer then it will probably have been anything but free! However, Anderson would argue that the cost of any individual activity – such as listening to a song or watching a video online – is small and getting smaller.

The second claim in the argument is that when something is entirely free, demand for that product escalates. There is something about 'free' that is very powerful. Think about the 'BOGOF' (buy one get one free) offers that you might have succumbed to, the free mobile phones that are given away with many mobile phone contracts, or any other free offers by which you may have been tempted.

The third claim in Anderson's argument is that if you give away something free then you don't have to be overly concerned about its

quality (beyond satisfying any relevant norms, laws and customs, of course – just because you are giving away free food doesn't mean to say that you can be any less careful over its ingredients or preparation). In the case of digital content, you can get away with less rigorous editing and lower production values if your audience is not paying for the content. Anderson cites YouTube as a good example of this phenomenon. Since people don't pay to watch videos on YouTube, they are more tolerant of their lower quality than if they were paying for them.

The final claim in the argument is that if you give away your information then you can – if you are clever enough and the content you are giving away attracts a sufficiently large or committed audience – make money around the thing being given away. There are some large and well-known examples of this phenomenon at work. Google, for example, gives away all its services but makes its money from advertising. Broadcast radio and television is free at the point of use (excepting some satellite and cable television stations, of course), but one way in which commercial broadcasters make money is by selling advertising space on their television or radio stations. So, attracting advertising revenue is one way in which you can make money when you give away your digital content.

To recap, Anderson's argument is founded on four claims:

1   *Technological*: the cost of producing, distributing and consuming content is falling and, in the case of the latter two, approaching zero.

2   *Psychological*: consumers like getting something free.

3   *Methodological or procedural*: as a creator or distributor of digital content, you don't have to make judgements on the quality of the content that you are producing or distributing (but see Part 5 of this block for a discussion of the legal, ethical and moral issues involved).

4   *Commercial*: you can make money out of distributing free content.

Is it really free?

You will notice that the final point of Anderson's argument is in fact about money, which might strike you as odd in a discussion of freedom. A quotation from the economist Arnold Kling introduces a new perspective on this apparent contradiction:

> A central economic paradox of our time is that information wants to be free, but people need to get paid.

Kling, 2002

So how do people get paid for their public goods? Looking specifically at created content, there are at least five ways:

1   By attracting advertising revenue.

2   By the government, through agencies such as The Arts Council.

3   Through patronage. In the fifteenth century, patronage was one of the major ways in which the arts were funded. This model could be redeveloped today using the power of the internet to connect artists with their patrons.

4   With funding from charities and corporate donations. Medical research is well endowed by this funding source; there are fewer well-known examples of where it is used to fund the creation of content.

5   Through the sale of items in some way associated with the content ('selling atoms not bits', as it has been called).

You will further explore the model set out in point 5 later in this part.

YouTube

I mentioned YouTube as an example of Anderson's argument that giving information away means that quality is less of an issue. However, the author Malcolm Gladwell, who writes for the *New Yorker* magazine, points out that YouTube ('a place to discover, watch, upload and share videos', to quote the YouTube website) has so far failed to make a profit (Gladwell, 2009). So whilst it is one of Anderson's major case studies, it apparently fails to support his claim about making money.

On this basis, it is interesting to delve a little deeper into the facts about YouTube. What are the arguments surrounding YouTube that Anderson and Gladwell use? YouTube, Anderson points out, hosts – and makes available for free download – vast amounts of video. Anyone can upload a video, anyone can download a video and YouTube doesn't have to judge the quality of the videos that it is hosting, beyond responding to users' complaints over offensiveness and legality. How does YouTube make money? From the advertising space that it sells on its website around the videos that people watch. Thus YouTube apparently follows Anderson's arguments for 'free' very closely.

However, Gladwell and others point out that YouTube doesn't make enough money to cover its costs. So what are its costs? In a report published by Credit Suisse in 2009, YouTube's major costs were identified as being first, providing and servicing the enormous storage and bandwidth required to host and serve all the videos that viewers want to watch; and second, licensing professionally produced content such as television programmes and films (Johnson, 2009). You may wonder why these costs are so high. Well, if it is free then everyone wants it (as Anderson argues), so YouTube is a very popular website. While the cost of hosting and streaming any one video is small and getting smaller, if you do that enough times – as YouTube has to – costs multiply and get very large. As for the reason why YouTube is purchasing licenses for television programmes and film: advertisers don't want their products associated with the vast majority of videos on YouTube (think how many videos in poor taste there could be on YouTube, even if you haven't watched any yourself). Thus the only way to attract significant advertising

revenue is for YouTube to purchase content alongside which advertisers are prepared to pay for advertisements.

All is not lost, however – there are many other examples where Chris Anderson's idea of 'free' does support viable businesses. I will explore some of these, and the business models under which they operate, later in this part.

2.6 Conclusion

In this session you have studied how creative works are protected by intellectual property law. I paid most attention to copyright law, since that is most relevant to the majority of creative works; you saw how copyright law is used to protect creative works and what you can do with copyrighted works under fair-use policies. I looked at the different levels of protection that are afforded to different industries and how the fashion industry thrives on an almost total lack of protection for its designs. Finally, I looked at how the internet is challenging this 'established' view of copyright being the protector of creative works through the ideas put forward by Chris Anderson, Cory Doctorow and others. They have proposed that computer technology and the internet have made it so easy to copy digital objects that information should be free and a public good.

This session should have helped you with the following learning outcomes.

- Summarise the different forms of legal protection that may be used to protect intellectual property (copyright, patents, trademarks and design rights).
- Understand some of the incentives in freely giving away digital content.
- Analyse the legitimacy of consumption of copyrighted material, both analogue (e.g. paper) and digital (e.g. film).

3 Stakeholders

In this session I will explore some of the complex issues that are involved in controlling access to, and making money from, people's intellectual endeavours through the creation of digital content. You learned in the previous session that there is a perception that information increasingly 'wants to be free'. In the activities in this session you will pursue this concept in particular and consider how money may still be made when information is given away.

To help in this analysis, I will consider which individuals and organisations have an interest, or stake, in a particular item of digital content. That is, who are the stakeholders?

3.1 Three stakeholder groups

A *stakeholder* is a person (or organisation) with an interest in or concern about something. For example, people who own shares in a company are stakeholders in that company. Customers of the company are also stakeholders because they have an interest in obtaining value for money from the products or services offered by the company.

Activity 10 (exploratory)

Think about who the stakeholders were in the last book you read, film you watched or piece of music you listened to.

Comment

I chose to think about who the stakeholders are in a book. The author of the book is a stakeholder because he or she had the idea for the book and wrote it, often with the aspiration of making a living through being a writer. Typically, authors don't sell their books directly to the public – that job is undertaken by a publisher. Publishers work with authors to write books for them so that they can sell those books to the public; therefore publishers are another stakeholder in the system.

I bought the last book I read from Amazon, whose business is selling books (and other items), so Amazon is another stakeholder in the book – as am I, as a purchaser of the book.

You may have identified other stakeholders in your answer to this activity.

Continuing with the book example, bookshops such as Amazon, Blackwells and Waterstones act as agents of publishers to distribute or sell books on the publisher's behalf; wholesalers and distributors act as intermediaries between printers and bookshops, and so on. But in a simple form, you can think of there being three types of stakeholder in a book: those who create the content (authors), those who distribute the content (publishers, bookshops, etc.) and those who consume the content (you and me, the readers).

More generally, the three groups of stakeholders in many of the creative industries – not just in publishing books – are as follows.

- *Creative stakeholders* such as artists, authors and composers create the content.

- *Commercial stakeholders* act as intermediaries between the creators of the content and the consumers. There are a multitude of different stakeholders that have an interest in exploiting content for commercial gain, ranging from publishers through distributors to broadcasters and beyond.

- *Consumer stakeholders* such as you and I read, listen to, watch and otherwise enjoy the content. Without this group of stakeholders, the commercial stakeholders would find it impossible to make any money from distributing and selling the content created by the creative stakeholders, and the creative stakeholders themselves would have no outlets for their work.

Figure 5 depicts the flow of digital content between the three stakeholder groups. This categorisation of stakeholders was used by Corrigan and Rogers (2005) in their paper on the economics of copyright. They identified these three stakeholder groups as having significantly different interests in copyright. Their analysis concluded that maximal benefits to society overall would be achieved when the sum of the benefits gained by the three stakeholder groups was at its maximum. They argued that the copyright system is a balancing act, dependent on a complex set of relationships between the three stakeholder groups, with market forces, new technologies and the legal system itself all affecting the benefits to

Figure 5   The three stakeholder domains (adapted from Umeh, 2007)

society that accrue through the protection of ideas and information by copyright law.

3.2 The digital supply chain

You may be familiar with the concept of a supply chain in a retail context, where the term is used to describe the sequence of organisations that are involved in the manufacture, distribution and sale of a particular product. The key distinction between this type of supply chain and a *digital* supply chain is that products passing along the latter are entirely digital in form and may well not exist in a physical form at any point during their passage along the digital supply chain. Content is created digitally and manipulated in various ways in order to get to the point at which the consumer can enjoy the digital content on their own digital device. Thus the *digital supply chain* describes how content is created, processed and used, and how it gets from the creator to the consumer via a number of intermediate processes and intermediaries.

Figure 6 shows the various links in the digital supply chain, beginning with production of the digital content by the creator – the creative stakeholder. The next four stages in the supply chain, from acquisition through processing and packaging to distribution, typically lie within the commercial domain. Traditionally, these are represented by publishers and other media companies. At the end of the digital supply chain lies the consumer. In the figure I have listed some of the processes that might take

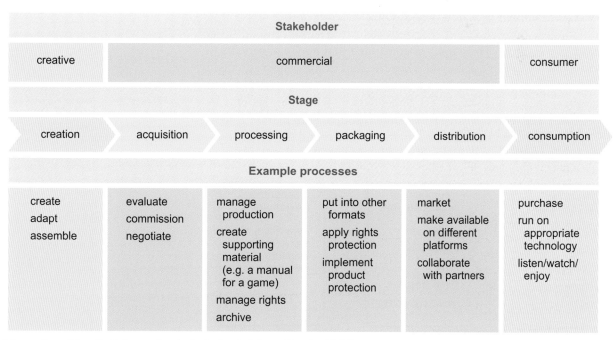

Figure 6   The digital supply chain (adapted from Umeh, 2007)

place at each stage of the digital supply chain. Note that these processes can involve technical transformation processes such as digitisation or compression as well as business processes such as contract negotiation and marketing.

I will now discuss some of the perspectives on the digital revolution of each of the three stakeholders, beginning with the content creators.

3.3 Creative stakeholders

Creative stakeholders – the content creators – drive the digital supply chain, representing all those individuals and organisations who are involved in creating digital content.

What impact has the digital revolution had on content creators? It has become easier, cheaper and quicker to create and reuse content as a consequence of the vast number of software applications that enable people to manipulate digital content (see Box 5).

Many would argue that in addition to making it cheaper and easier for people to create digital content, the digital revolution has also increased the pool of content creators. Put simply, new digital technologies are enabling people to create who would not have done so otherwise.

Box 5 Creating digital content: examples

Below are three examples of software applications that make it easier for people to create digital content.

1 *Sibelius* is music notation software that can be used to write music. First released in 1993 for Acorn computers, it has developed to become one of the leading software applications for composers and musicians – young and old, amateur and professional.

2 For images, *Adobe Photoshop* is image manipulation software that can be used to manipulate digital images in almost every conceivable way. Photoshop has a longer history than Sibelius, having been first released in 1988 for the Apple Macintosh.

3 *GarageBand* is a software application that supports the creation of music and podcasts. It can record, mix and play back several audio tracks. This has enabled many 'garage bands' to record their own music, mix it and release it to wider audiences, something that would not have been possible before the digital revolution. In the days of analogue music, it would simply have been too expensive for most bands to hire a recording studio so that they could record their music.

Alongside the ease with which digital content can be created goes the ease with which it can be copied – hence the need for a system that will protect digital content from illegal dissemination. At least, commercial stakeholders generally perceive this need: digital protection is clearly important so that they can realise a return on their investments and assets. In contrast, authors, composers and songwriters may have more diverse views, ranging from those who side with the commercial stakeholders in wanting their creations to be protected, to those (perhaps new artists in particular) who are happy with any form of distribution of their works in order to create and cultivate an audience.

This point about the need for content protection gets to the heart of copyright and intellectual property issues. The need perceived by content creators for protection of their work has had a long history (see Box 6).

Box 6 The march king

John Philip Sousa, the US bandleader and composer, was born in 1854. Sousa was a prolific composer of songs and operettas, but he is best known as a composer of military marches. Among his most famous compositions are *Semper Fidelis* (the official march of the US Marine Corps), *The Liberty Bell* and *The Stars and Stripes Forever*.

Sousa was also a prolific writer. In 1906, he wrote an article called 'The Menace of Mechanical Music' in which he railed against the reproduction of music by machines. At the time Sousa wrote the article, the primary means of music reproduction were musical boxes, pianos controlled by piano rolls and primitive phonographs. Sousa argued two main points. The first was the social decline caused by a reduction in the practice of amateur music-making. Before mechanically or electronically reproduced music became commonly available, the practice of singing songs around a piano for evening entertainment was a common pastime. However, more pertinent to this part of TU100 was Sousa's second point, which was the threat that mechanical music reproduction posed to composers' rights. Sousa wrote:

> Do they not realize that if the accredited composers, who have come into vogue by reason of merit and labor, are refused a just reward for their efforts, a condition is almost sure to arise where all incentive to further creative work is lacking, and compositions will no longer flow from their pens; or where they will be compelled to refrain from publishing their compositions at all, and control them in manuscript?

Sousa, 1906, p. 284

Creators and consumers

It is interesting to consider the nature of the relationship between creators of content and their audiences – the content consumers – in the internet age. Nowadays few authors, musicians or songwriters, except perhaps the most established, create their content, give it to a publisher, then sit back and wait for the royalties to roll in while they are creating their next work. For many authors, social media websites such as blogs have replaced promotional tours. Authors publish extracts of their next book online as works in progress and musicians put snippets of their performances online as free downloads. One reason for doing this is to maintain and build the relationship they have with their audiences: gaining feedback and comments from their fans and creating a sense of anticipation for their next work.

Modern content creators have a much closer relationship with their audiences than did those who worked before the advent of the internet – except perhaps before the Industrial Revolution, when artefacts and people were less mobile and so it was more common to know the (analogue) content creator personally. Moreover, content creators – particularly those working in audio and video – have to be comfortable with the idea of working with multiple formats, delivering content through multiple channels to consumers who have many choices over how they receive and use content.

Giving it all away: the creator's perspective

The creative industries are in a state of flux, with many different business models being explored to make money from content that some people say can't (or shouldn't) be sold. One type of business model is based, as you saw, on the notion of giving digital content away free.

Activity 11 (self-assessment)

Earlier I listed five ways of making money by giving away digital content. What were they?

In the remaining activities in this session you will explore (i) the different stakeholder perspectives on the 'give it away free' class of business model and (ii) specific ways of making money in this model by selling associated items.

Activity 12 (exploratory)

Put yourself in the position of a musician who creates digital works for a living: a creative stakeholder. How might you benefit financially from giving away some or all of your work? What questions or concerns would you have about this idea?

Comment

Here is my answer. Yours may make different points.

Giving away 'tasters' of my music on my website might attract a wider audience who would be willing to pay for the complete works. But if I give away all my music (as Coldplay did with their 2009 album *LeftRightLeftRight*) could I make enough money from selling T-shirts? Even if I could, would that turn me into a T-shirt designer and not a singer/songwriter? What would my publisher think? Would I even need a publisher any more? Would giving all my music away mean that I might be able to attract more people to buy tickets for my live performances?

In answer to some of the questions I posed in the previous activity, at least in part: T-shirts are big business (for instance, US citizens spend around $40 billion a year on decorated clothing), so there is the potential to make a living from this (Thompson, 2008). And the amount of money spent on live performances is growing (up 16% in 2006 to a record $3.6 billion in the USA) – 92% of the Rolling Stones' $150.6 million revenue in 2006 came from ticket sales (Anderson, 2007).

Links to Thompson's article and a reply to it can be found in the online resources page associated with this part.

3.4 Commercial stakeholders

The rapid pace of change in digital technologies aimed at the consumer has helped to create vibrant markets for new products and services for digital content, as well as new challenges for commercial stakeholders. This is particularly evident in the music industry.

As evidence of the rapid development of new markets, the music industry's revenues from digital music stores such as iTunes increased from being negligible in 2003 to $4.2 billion in 2009, which represents 27% of the total global revenue for the music industry. In the USA, revenues from digital music increased from virtually nothing to approximately 40% of the music market in the space of eight years. iTunes is a particularly interesting example of a commercial stakeholder in the digital music industry: it is now the biggest music retailer in the USA, accounting for 25% of the overall music market.

iTunes

iTunes is an online retailer of digital media that is operated by Apple, the computer manufacturer. It opened for business on 28 April 2003 selling, as its name suggests, music that could be downloaded and played on the company's iPod range of music players. This created a link between the hardware that Apple sold and the digital content that could be played on that hardware. Apple took the approach that the more content there was available for iPods, the more sales of both iPods and music there would be.

The iTunes pricing model was simple: all individual songs were sold for the same price and there was no subscription fee, which made it considerably less complicated than many of its competitors at the time. To begin with music was encoded using Apple's own DRM system, FairPlay, which encrypts music encoded in the Advanced Audio Coding (AAC) format in order to prevent it from being played on unauthorised computers.

The iTunes music store has been enormously successful: in less than a decade, it has grown from nothing to being the most popular online music store in the world, selling its 10 billionth song download on 24 February 2010, less than seven years after it opened. Worldwide, it now accounts for 70% of online digital music sales, making it the largest legal music retailer in the world.

In 2007 Steve Jobs, the CEO of Apple, published an online article called *Thoughts on Music* in which he said:

> Why would the big four music companies agree to let Apple and others distribute their music without using DRM systems to protect it? The simplest answer is because DRMs haven't worked, and may never work, to halt music piracy.

Jobs, 2007

This initiated a change in Apple's policy such that some music downloads (initially from EMI and certain other independent labels) became available without the restrictions on their use that was enforced by FairPlay (in other words, without DRM). The files were encoded in an enhanced AAC format under the brand name iTunes Plus. This was extended to all iTunes' digital music during 2009, so now all the music that can be downloaded from iTunes is unprotected by FairPlay.

This is in contrast to other media and file formats that iTunes has added to its catalogue during the course of its short life. In addition to digital music, iTunes sells music videos, films, television shows and audio books, although many of these are not available outside the USA. The very successful App Store is also part of iTunes. Apps are small software applications that can be run on some of Apple's handheld

products such as the iPhone, iPod Touch and iPad. All these formats are DRM protected.

Music piracy

You may be surprised to learn that the growth in the sale of music through downloading (in various forms) is not offsetting the decline in music sales in physical formats. In its annual report on the state of digital music, the International Federation of the Phonographic Industry (IFPI, the organisation that represents the interests of the recording industry worldwide) reported that in 2009, global music sales fell for the tenth year running. This trade organisation, as do many others in the recording and allied industries, places the blame for this decline in sales at the door of piracy. As the report states, 'Digital piracy remains a huge barrier to market growth' (IFPI, 2010, p. 3). The foreword to the report by the then Chairman and Chief Executive of the IFPI, John Kennedy, concludes by saying 'To unlock the enormous potential of digital music, we have to address piracy both on P2P [peer-to-peer] networks and in other forms. That is where, today, we look to governments for action' (IFPI, ibid.).

Commercial stakeholders having appealed to governments to help the recording industry out of their predicament, what are they doing themselves? Both the recording and broadcasting industries have a three-pronged approach to tackling piracy (BBC, 2010; IFPI, 2010):

1   Digital rights management – a technical approach to the problem of piracy.

2   Education, to improve people's awareness and understanding of copyright legislation. You may have seen the notices that are played at the beginning of films – both in the cinema and on DVDs – that warn against piracy and the illicit copying or recording of copyrighted material.

3   Enacting and then enforcing anti-piracy legislation. A recent example of legislation in this area in the UK is the Digital Economy Act 2010, which you saw previously in this part.

Activity 13 (exploratory)

In this second part of the stakeholders activity, put yourself in the position of a book publisher: a commercial stakeholder. How might you feel if one of your authors came to you and said that they wanted to give away the next book in their (your) bestselling series online, as well as selling paper copies?

Comment

Here is my answer. Yours may make different points.

Give away the 'family silver'? You must be joking! Would we make money by selling merchandise instead? But how are our distributors and retailers going to cope if we ask them to start selling merchandise such as T-shirts, mugs and fluffy toys instead of books? They don't have the facilities to sell those things – the merchandise won't fit on the bookshelves and the shops don't have changing rooms.

What else might be in it for us? Presumably publicity – we might sell more copies of this and other books the author has written, perhaps even books by some of our other authors.

But wouldn't it harm the sales of the paper copy of this book? Why buy a paper copy of a book when you can download a free copy of the book? What can we add to the paid-for version of the book to encourage people to buy it? Perhaps a taster such as the first chapter of the next book in the series.

Might this lead to a new line in selling ebooks? But then what is my role to be? Do I even have one?

One of the reasons that authors and publishers give away copies of their books electronically is to increase the visibility of their work. A small study by Hilton and Wiley (2010) looked at the impact that a free digital version of a book had on sales of the print version of the book for a short while after the free version was available. The study found a correlation between free digital books being made available and a short-term increase in sales of the print version of the book.

Disintermediation

The word *disintermediation* can be broken down: 'dis' (removing) those who 'inter-mediate' (negotiate between). It is a term most used in the financial world, where it refers to the trend for customers to stop using middlemen such as bankers and brokers in their financial transactions, and instead to deal with the supplier direct. For example, telephone call centres and then the internet have led to a large rise in the number of people who book their insurance or take out a mortgage directly with an insurance company or mortgage lender, without going through an intermediary such as an insurance broker or mortgage advisor.
There are several reasons why disintermediation has happened in the financial sector, including deregulation of the financial services sector, but new technologies – particularly widespread use of the internet – have had a significant impact on this industry.

Some commentators argue that the internet will have a similar impact on digital content. With the advent of the internet, it is now much easier for

digital content creators to reach their audiences than it used to be. Likewise, it is much easier for consumers to find and get access to digital content than in the past. So, they ask, what of the middlemen – the commercial stakeholders – in this industry? Do they have a future or will disintermediation take place in the digital media industry too, leading to commercial stakeholders going out of business while creators and consumers deal directly with each other?

3.5 Consumer stakeholders

Consumers are the *raison d'être* for the digital supply chain and the creation of the vast majority of digital content. Their position at the end of the digital supply chain may appear to belittle their existence, but without an audience few artistic works would be created and none would be sold. It is the consumers who read, listen to or watch digital content and, through their activity and purchasing decisions, generate the revenue that drives the whole digital media industry. Yet it is this group – as in some other industries – that is also often overlooked by the other stakeholder groups, except perhaps when their revenue is threatened by the actions of consumers.

The near-universal use of communication and information technologies has made it possible for people to get online on a global scale, and potential consumers are increasingly finding that content is apparently readily available. So what do most consumers want from digital content – whatever type, in whatever format? They want it preferably now and ideally free. And once they have it, they want the convenience of being able to do what they want with it. Unfortunately, some of the things that consumers might want to do with digital content contravene copyright legislation and others they are prevented from doing by DRM.

Activity 14 (self-assessment)

Table 1 is adapted from a report called *Copycats? Digital Consumers in the Online Age*, published by the Strategic Advisory Board for Intellectual Property Policy (SABIP, 2009, p. 64). The table lists some ways in which digital content can be acquired physically or virtually.

I have started to fill in Table 1 to describe the legitimacy of digital content use. Complete the entries as best you can.

Note that copyright legislation is changing, meaning some activities that were legal may not be in the future and vice versa. Therefore it is always best to confirm your knowledge and understanding of the law with an expert, typically a member of the legal profession.

Table 1   Ways in which digital content can be obtained

Source of digital content	Legitimacy of digital content use
Buy it in a physical format from a physical shop, or rent it from a video store or library, then copy to a computer.	If you buy, rent or borrow a copy of digital content (or analogue content such as a book) then that is entirely legal. The problem comes if you then copy the content. Depending upon how much you copy, you might be breaching copyright law.
Buy it as a counterfeit copy from a market, pub or 'friend', and then copy to a computer.	This is illegal since your source is a counterfeit copy of the content.
Listen to it on the Web via a 'subscription' service (such as the most recent incarnation of Napster) – essentially 'rent' the content.	
Find it via a 'content' blog that has posted it for 'sampling'.	
Find and copy it to your computer from a peer-to-peer file-sharing network (BitTorrent etc.).	
Copy broadcasts from a television using a DVD recorder or hard drive.	

Peer-to-peer file sharing

File sharing via peer-to-peer networks is usually cited as a major factor in the decline in music sales – a decline of 30% between 2004 and 2009 (IFPI, 2010). The evidence would appear to be incontrovertible: more than 60% of internet traffic consists of consumers sharing music, films, books and games (Oberholzer-Gee and Strumpf, 2010), and a recent investigation found that in a sample of just over 1000 different files that were available on the BitTorrent file-sharing system, only 1% of the files did *not* infringe copyright (Sahi and Felton, 2010). Interestingly, music accounted for only 10% of the files that were being shared. Nearly half the files in the sample (46%) were films and television shows, and another 14% were games and software.

What of consumers' behaviour as influenced by the law? Months after Sweden introduced anti-piracy laws in 1999, there was a dramatic rise in music sales in the country. At the time of writing, the Digital Economy Act 2010 has become law but it is too early to anticipate what its impact will be on consumers' behaviour in the UK.

Earlier in TU100 you explored some of the impacts and implications of the rise of Web 2.0 and social computing. In essence what has happened with Web 2.0 is that the wider population have become not just passive

consumers of content created by others but active creators of content themselves. Whether it is writing blogs, creating Facebook pages, taking photographs that we put on Flickr or filming videos that we put on YouTube, we all create our own content. How has this changed the digital content landscape? Unfortunately, in addition to originating our own content, there is a tendency to reuse other people's content too – including that which is copyrighted.

YouTube's 'fingerprinting' technology

In order to protect itself from litigation over breach of copyright, YouTube has developed video 'fingerprinting' technology that will, much like conventional fingerprints, identify unique features of video clips so that YouTube can prevent copyrighted video clips from being uploaded without permission. In a novel twist on this story, YouTube is now employing this technology to support revenue from advertising in two different ways:

- Firstly, it identifies videos that already contain advertisements – about one third of these are unauthorised uploads of copyrighted material. Instead of blocking these uploads, YouTube is now sharing the revenue obtained from showing these advertisements with the copyright owner.

- Secondly, rather than blocking the upload of other kinds of copyrighted material, YouTube associates display advertisements with this material, again sharing the revenue with the copyright owner.

Both these methods are examples of the 'Freemium' model, whereby a technology – YouTube – that is free to use (and thus is very widely used) nevertheless makes money through revenue obtained from a small proportion of its users. Stakeholders hope that YouTube may even become profitable by tapping into these ways of making money (Rosenblatt, 2010b).

Activity 15 (exploratory)

In this third part of the stakeholders activity, put yourself in the position of a consumer. How might you feel if one of the independent film producers whose films you enjoy watching started giving away their films free on the internet?

Comment

Here is my answer. Yours may make different points.

Wow, free? Do I really get to watch the film for nothing? What's the catch? But if I don't buy something from them, my favourite film producer might not be able to make another film. However, I really don't need yet another T-shirt! Perhaps I should pay to go to a film festival and

see a live screening of the film instead. But tickets are expensive and I can download an illegal copy of films shown at the festival online.

In the previous activity and two related ones in this session, you put yourself in the position of three stakeholders in order to determine their perspective on a new business model for making money from created works: give the content away free and sell other items (T-shirts, mugs, tickets, future content, the same content but in different formats, etc.) instead. This three-part activity could be repeated for several other business models, such as a subscription model (where you charge subscribers a fixed monthly or annual fee, supplying them with new content at regular intervals) or patronage (where a few wealthy benefactors support artists directly). You might like to think about these potential scenarios from the three stakeholder perspectives.

3.6   Conclusion

In this session you studied the perspectives on the digital revolution of three different groups who have an interest in the digital supply chain: the creative stakeholders, the commercial stakeholders and the consumers. In a series of activities you examined their perspectives on what might be described as a business model of the digital age – giving it away free – and you discovered how, despite the name, money can in fact be made from this model.

This session should have helped you with the following learning outcomes.

- Understand some of the incentives in freely giving away digital content.
- Demonstrate an awareness of the different stakeholders involved in the digital supply chain and their different perspectives on copyright and digital rights management.
- Demonstrate an awareness of the legal, business and ethical contexts for the distribution of digital works.
- Analyse the legitimacy of consumption of copyrighted material, both analogue (e.g. paper) and digital (e.g. film).
- Analyse a given business model from the perspectives of the three stakeholders (creative, commercial and consumer) in the digital supply chain.

4 Regulation of behaviour

Previously in this part you have seen how laws (such as copyright legislation) and technologies (such as DRM) can both influence people's access to and consumption of digital content. In this session I want to consider further how these and other factors can influence behaviour.

In 1999 Lawrence Lessig, a US professor of law, published a book called *Code and Other Laws of Cyberspace* in which he put forward a model of how people's behaviour on the internet is regulated or constrained by four main forces: laws, social norms, market forces and architecture. In this session I will describe Lessig's model and use it to help you understand in particular the influences on people's consumption of digital content.

> There are many ways to think about constitutional law and the limits it may impose on governmental regulation. I want to think about it from the perspective of someone who is regulated or constrained. That someone regulated is represented by this (pathetic) dot – a creature (you or me) subject to the different constraints that might regulate it.
>
> Lessig, 1999, p. 86

Lessig describes a person as a 'dot', perhaps to illustrate their size and significance in relation to the internet. In Figure 7 I have redrawn the dot as a person, surrounded by the four constraints that Lessig says operate on them.

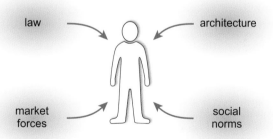

Figure 7   Lessig's four constraints on behaviour (based on Lessig, 1999)

I will now look at each of these four constraints in turn.

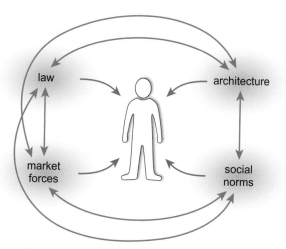

4.1   Law

Laws provide a framework through which governments prescribe what is acceptable behaviour and what is not. Laws act as a threat: if we don't follow the law, there is a risk that we will be found out and punished. Lessig illustrates this through the example of smoking. Laws regulate smoking to the extent that adults may only smoke in certain places and cigarettes are not supposed to be sold to children. If someone smokes indoors in a public place, or if retailers sell cigarettes to children, then they can be prosecuted.

Laws can be just as effective in influencing online behaviour.

Activity 16 (self-assessment)

Give an example of a law that influences people's online behaviour.

4.2   Social norms

Social norms are the conventions – rarely written down – that groups use to identify appropriate and inappropriate behaviours, attitudes, values and beliefs. In other words, they are the social conventions by which societies operate. Peer pressure is one way in which social norms exert their influence – peer pressure being the influence exerted by a peer group to encourage someone to change their behaviour, attitudes, values or beliefs in order that they conform more closely to the group's norms. The desire for approval, to fit in with the group, can be a powerful force in influencing what people wear, what they say or how they behave.

So, our perceptions of social norms strongly influence how we behave as individuals. Unfortunately, these perceptions are not always accurate. For example, we may assume that others are behaving in a less healthy and socially responsible fashion than is actually the case. Studies of US students have shown that they overestimate how frequently and how heavily their peers drink alcohol. This impression can lead students to drink more alcohol themselves in a mistaken attempt to match what they perceive to be the group norm. This research has led to a *social norms approach* being adopted in some contexts (such as health campaigns), involving disseminating information on what is actually going on (what the social norms are as opposed to what they are perceived to be) in the hope of modifying people's behaviour (McAlaney et al., 2010).

Activity 17 (exploratory)

Can you think of any social norms that have had some influence over your or someone else's behaviour?

Comment

I thought of the social norms surrounding drink driving. Not that long ago – perhaps 40 years or so – drink driving was far more socially acceptable in the UK than it is now. Many people would have thought nothing of driving home from the pub, for example, with several drinks inside them. Now, however, it is largely seen as socially unacceptable to drink and drive, and far fewer people do.

This change in behaviour has been partly due to awareness-raising via campaigns such as the THINK! campaign, which has been run by the UK Department for Transport since 2000. Many people will remember this campaign for its hard-hitting advertisements of the potential consequences of drink driving that appeared on television around Christmas. As the THINK! campaign website states:

> The THINK! campaign is not about the motorist as such, or the pedestrians, or cyclists, motor cyclists, etc. It is about people, about the citizen, about each and all of us. It is about how we all use our roads safely, whether we happen to be motoring, walking, cycling or whatever. This is mainly to build a mood of "we're all in it together" to have greater effect.

Department of Transport, 2010

In other words, the THINK! campaign is about creating and changing social norms.

You may well have thought of other social norms, such as the peer pressure and social norms that operate amongst children and teenagers, or the style of dress at work.

Social norms can influence online behaviour too.

Activity 18 (exploratory)

Give an example of a social norm that influences people's online behaviour.

Comment

One example might be peer pressure amongst schoolchildren to be active on certain social media sites, e.g. to have a Facebook page.

Social norms and the law

Figure 7 showed each of the four forces acting independently on the 'dot' in the centre of the figure, but the forces interact with each other too. Consider the example I gave in Activity 17 of the social norms around drink driving. Alongside campaigns to raise public awareness, the

enforcement of laws proscribing drink driving has also played a significant role in influencing social norms around drink driving.

Social norms and the law interact in the following ways (Schultz, 2006, pp. 10–11).

- The law can influence social norms. The existence of a law or the passing of a new law can change people's behaviour to the point that a new social norm develops. Active enforcement of a law can, aside from the direct effect on the people concerned, underline the importance of taking particular behaviours seriously.

- Social norms can encourage compliance with the law. It has even been argued that social norms have a greater effect in securing compliance with the law than official enforcement of the law.

- The reverse is also true: social norms are so powerful that they can discourage compliance with the law (for example, driving in excess of the speed limit).

- Social norms can still operate in the absence of a law.

Thus social norms and the law interact in sometimes complementary and sometimes contradictory ways.

Copynorms

'Copynorms' is a term that was popularised by Mark Schultz, a US academic lawyer who specialises in intellectual property law. Schultz (2006, p. 2) defines *copynorms* as the social norms regarding the copying, distribution and use of created works. He argues that copynorms can ameliorate, extend or undermine the effect of copyright law. Therefore, understanding copynorms is essential to understanding fully how copyright law affects society.

Below I will look briefly at a number of different copynorms, including some that attempt to change or replace copyright law.

Creative Commons licences

Creative Commons licences, as you learned in Block 3 Part 5, are an attempt to replace copyright protection with a less restrictive protection that is somewhere between full copyright protection and releasing a work into the public domain, while still being enforceable in a court of law. In effect, the Creative Commons licenses are attempting to create a new norm.

Activity 19 (exploratory)

A short audio on the subject of Creative Commons is provided in the resources page associated with this part on the TU100 website. When convenient, listen to this audio and make some brief notes.

Similarly, the open source software community has created its own set of norms. Indeed, if someone violates these norms by trying to profit from open source software then they run the risk of being cast out by that community.

Internet copynorms

This term refers to activities such as search engine indexing and archiving on the internet, which could raise copyright issues but have not been challenged. Technically, search engine companies that take copies of web pages so that they can build indexes of them are in breach of copyright. Even more so is the Internet Archive, which maintains an archive of pages published on the Web. The Internet Archive offers free access to 150 billion archived web pages as well a digital library of books, films and music. The archive of web pages is known as the 'Wayback Machine' because it provides a way of retrieving old versions of a website. You used the Wayback Machine in Block 3 Part 4.

Google, having built its multi-billion dollar business on copying and indexing web pages, did encounter considerable opposition when it proposed to do the same for its Google Books project in which it is working with libraries and publishers to scan out-of-copyright and some in-copyright books and make them available online. This demonstrates the different norms of the online and print publishing worlds – at least in the early twenty-first century.

Continuing this theme, have you ever thought about the copyright implications of quoting other people's email in replies or when forwarding messages? Probably not, but apparently this was debated in the early days of the internet. Now, everyone just takes these practices as normal – for without them, the internet and World Wide Web would cease to function effectively. Thus new internet copynorms have been created.

Home recording

Home recording and copying of music became significant with the invention of the cassette recorder and has expanded with the ever-increasing diversity of formats and devices for storing and playing back audio and video material. Many people use the recording capabilities of video recorders (first analogue and now digital) for time-shifting purposes (that is, to view or listen to later on) and to build libraries of their own favourite programmes and films that are broadcast on television. Much of this home recording is of questionable legality although it is widely considered to be entirely acceptable.

File sharing

It can be argued that file sharing of digital content and software over the internet has been encouraged by the home recording copynorms I've just mentioned. If you are used to being able to record a film from broadcast television, why should you not you copy a film from the internet using a

file-sharing program? Many people do not believe file sharing to be wrong and the widespread nature of file sharing reinforces this norm. Indeed, the activities of trade bodies such as the International Federation of the Phonographic Industry, which argue strongly against file sharing (see for example IFPI, 2010), may inadvertently be encouraging the file-sharing copynorm by highlighting the widespread nature of the practice, thus reinforcing the message that 'everyone else is doing it (and not being caught) so why shouldn't I?'

4.3 Market forces

Put simply, markets dictate that we don't get access to something (we are unable to make a purchase) unless we offer a token (money) in exchange. This indicates a fairly obvious connection between market forces and behaviour: if you don't have the money, you can't access the goods. So the price of a product can be used to regulate behaviour – witness the debate about raising the tax on alcohol or banning supermarkets from selling alcohol at or below cost price. Of course, the law is involved here too – a tax on alcohol is attempting to regulate behaviour – but the way the law operates in this instance is through market forces, not by constraining or banning the consumption of alcohol.

However, if the price is too high then this can be an incentive to turn to alternative means of obtaining the product – legitimate or otherwise. For example, high prices at online music stores, it could be argued, are an incentive to turn to alternative methods of obtaining music such as file sharing or ripping media borrowed from friends or a public lending library.

When he introduced the iTunes music store in 2003, Apple's CEO Steve Jobs turned this argument on its head. He argued that people who were downloading songs illegally by file sharing were effectively working for less than the minimum wage compared to the cost of downloading (and paying for) the same songs from Apple. By downloading songs from iTunes, you were assured of the quality and legitimacy of the song – neither of which, Jobs argued, were you assured of if you obtained them from a file-sharing site.

> Well, let me give you an observation that's really interesting. If you go to Kazaa and you try to find a song, you don't find a single song. You find 50 versions of that song, and you have to pick which one to try to download, and usually it's not a very good connection. You have to try another one, and by the time you finally get a clean version of the song you want, it takes about 15 minutes. If you do the math, that means that you're spending an hour to download four songs that you could buy for under $4 from Apple, which means you're working for under minimum wage.

You can read CNN's full interview with Steve Jobs by going to the online resources page associated with this part.

Steve Jobs, quoted in CNN (2003)

The Times **paywall**

Market forces can regulate other behaviour on the internet too. In July 2010 *The Times* and the *Sunday Times*, having been freely available on the internet for some years, were placed behind a 'paywall'. (By analogy with a firewall, a paywall blocks access to a website until a payment is received.) In effect, these two newspapers were turned into subscription publications, although a subscription could last for as little as 24 hours while giving access to the whole website for that period.

In November 2010 the first statistics on the project were released. Based on these statistics, most commentators argued that the online audience for *The Times* newspaper had fallen by more than 90% to 105 000 subscribers. While *The Times* is now making money from these subscribers, the vast audience of the internet is lost to them, which reduces advertising revenue. However, there is a flip side to this: the audience of subscribers is more valuable to advertisers, since they tend to be better off and read more of the newspaper than those who visited the newspaper when access was free.

Apart from the revenue implications, a paywall also blocks what the Editor of *The Times* called the 'internet conversation'. Journalists who write for *The Times* used to benefit from an extended group of followers, who might comment on their articles, recommend them to friends on social networking sites and so on. This may still be happening behind the paywall, but the conversation is amongst a smaller cross section of society – those who are willing to pay for their content.

4.4 Architecture

It is not hard to see how physical architecture – the built environment – shapes our behaviour. As a very simple example, if a building has steep steps at the entrance and no other way in, it is difficult for a wheelchair user to enter the building unaided. This influences wheelchair users' behaviour with respect to entering the building. As another example, a major airline once noticed that passengers on Monday morning flights were frustrated with the length of time it took to retrieve their bags. As a result, it started parking these flights further away from the baggage reclaim lounge, meaning that by the time the passengers got there their bags had arrived. The complaints stopped.

Activity 20 (exploratory)

Give an example of another physical architectural feature that influences behaviour.

Comment

I thought of speed bumps, placed in roads to encourage drivers to slow down.

When Lessig (1999) uses the term 'architecture' in relation to the digital world, he is talking about the software and hardware infrastructure that composes the internet: the 'shape' of the internet, you might say. This 'digital' architecture constrains what is possible, easy or difficult to achieve on the internet. While the constraints may vary, they manifest themselves as conditions on what you can and can't do and so influence your online behaviour. Examples include the use of passwords (or not) to gain access to computer networks, software that blocks access to certain websites, and the constraints imposed by DRM.

Activity 21 (exploratory)

Give another example of a digital architectural feature that influences people's online behaviour.

Comment

I thought of software licences that have security codes specific to the computer for which the software is licensed, so the software cannot be run if the computer is replaced.

I will conclude this discussion of Lessig's constraints on behaviour by noting that in Figure 7, each constraint is shown as being distinct. However, as the previous discussion has shown, the four constraints on behaviour interact: they can reinforce or undermine each other, and thus they are very much interdependent on one other. So in actuality, the figure should look rather more like Figure 8, with each of the four constraints affecting and being affected by the other three constraints and, in turn, affecting the person in the middle.

Activity 22 (self-assessment)

Give an example of a digital architectural feature that supports an aspect of the law.

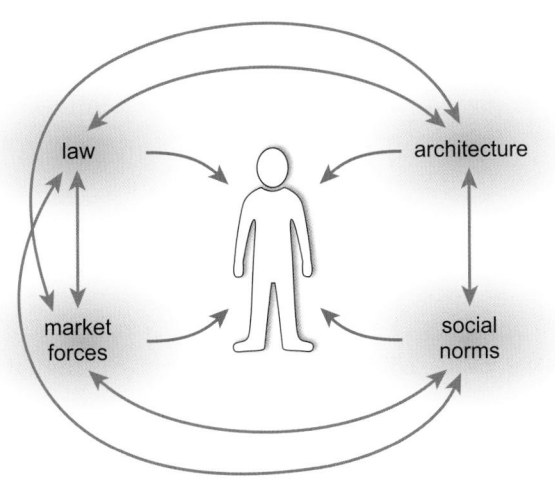

Figure 8   Lessig's four constraints on behaviour, showing the complexity of the interactions between each of the constraints and the person who they regulate

4.5   Conclusion

In this session I looked at Lessig's model of the four constraints on our behaviour with respect to digital content: law, social norms, market forces and architecture.

This session should have helped you with the following learning outcomes.

- Understand the constraints that affect behaviour according to Lessig (law, social norms, market forces and architecture) and how they interact, reinforcing or undermining each other.

- Identify the constraints (according to Lessig) on behaviour with respect to the consumption of digital content.

The copyright debate

5

This session (including the remaining activities in this part of TU100) is delivered online. It can be found in the resources page associated with this part on the TU100 website.

Summary

In this part of TU100 I began by looking at DRM and how it is used to protect digital content. I then discussed what DRM is intended to protect – that is, intellectual property – looking at what it is, how it has been protected in the past and how it is being protected now. I looked at some of the ways in which the internet has changed the status quo that used to exist between those who create new ideas and content, the publishers and others who distribute it, and those who use or enjoy creative works – you and me. You discovered that there are powerful arguments for the position that information is a public good and is not something that can or should be charged for in a system where the cost of duplicating and distributing information is vanishingly small. In other words, information should be free.

Next, I looked at the various stakeholders that have an interest in digital content and the way in which this content can be thought of as passing from one to another along a supply chain, analogous to the supply chains for manufacturing physical goods. You considered the different perspective of each of the stakeholders on digital content, particularly with respect to giving information away free. I introduced Lessig's model of constraints on behaviour and you saw how these constraints apply to access to and consumption of digital content, and how they are interlinked. Finally, you listened to a debate that explored many of the issues introduced in this part, and considered how your own opinions may have changed and how your opinions on the issues raised in this part compare to those of your peers on the module.

The final part of this block will consider some of the legal, ethical and moral issues that have come to the fore with the development of the internet, including freedom of speech and how online actions can have real-world effects. Part 5 is presented online, so when you have finished looking at the web resources associated with this part you should go on to start studying it.

Answers to self-assessment activities

Activity 2

Having 409 player keys means that each manufacturer of DVD players need only know the keys that they include in their DVD players, so any security breach is likely to affect only the keys of a single manufacturer. The affected keys can be removed from the table in all DVDs produced after the security breach has been detected.

Activity 3

(a) The robust watermark would remain on the copy. The fragile watermark would be absent.

(b) An old, non-SDMI-compliant player would lack the watermark-checking process and would simply play a pirated CD.

Activity 4

As you learned in Block 1 Part 2, the process of taking a digital representation of an analogue quantity usually involves loss of accuracy.

Activity 5

(a) *Patents* are typically awarded to inventors who create a novel piece of work (usually a physical object). The patent gives the inventor exclusive rights to produce that work and profit from sales of the work for a limited period of time. In exchange, the inventor makes public the design and working of the item. If a piece of work is to be patented then it must be original and novel, and must not be an obvious development of an existing idea.

Trademarks are used by companies and other organisations to identify their brand. A trademark must be registered as belonging to a particular organisation and then cannot legally be used by any other organisation. Once registered, trademarks have to be renewed; if they are not then they are deemed to have lapsed and can be used by anyone.

Copyright applies to any intellectual or artistic work that can be realised in some form, for example books, plays, dances and concerts, films, music and audio recordings, paintings, drawings, sculptures and photographs. Under copyright law, the creator of a piece of work is given the exclusive right to benefit from their work for a period of time, after which the work is made freely available to all.

(b) A licence is a mechanism for giving permission. For example, if you wanted to put on a play that was under copyright, you would need to obtain a licence from the copyright owner permitting you to do so.

Activity 6

In fact, precisely the reverse is true – the industries that are intellectual property intensive are very small in relation to the industries that have little intellectual property protection. In other words, large industries typically have low levels of protection.

Activity 9

The 'laws' in the quotation are the laws of intellectual property – in the digital realm, these are the laws governing the protection and exploitation of digital content.

The 'locks' in the quotation are digital rights management technologies, which aim to keep digital content safely under lock and key.

Activity 11

The five ways I listed of making money by giving away digital content were:

1   advertising

2   government funding

3   patronage – connecting artists with private patrons

4   funding via charities and corporate donations

5   the sale of items associated with the content.

Activity 14

Table 2 shows my completed answer.

Table 2   Ways in which digital content can be obtained and their legitimacy

Source of digital content	Legitimacy of digital content use
Buy it in a physical format from a physical shop, or rent it from a video store or library, then copy to a computer.	If you buy, rent or borrow a copy of digital content (or analogue content such as a book) then that is entirely legal. The problem comes if you then copy the content. Depending upon how much you copy, you might be breaching copyright law.
Buy it as a counterfeit copy from a market, pub or 'friend', and then copy to a computer.	This is illegal since your source is a counterfeit copy of the content.
Listen to it on the Web via a 'subscription' service (such as Napster) – essentially 'rent' the content.	This is legal – there is no copying involved – and the source is legitimate.
Find it via a 'content' blog that has posted it for 'sampling'.	If the content is posted as a sample then presumably it can be downloaded and used legitimately, subject to any restrictions that may have been advised in the blog.
Find and copy it to your computer from a peer-to-peer file-sharing network (BitTorrent etc.).	This could be legal and the copy of the file might be legitimate, but peer-to-peer networks are notorious among the film and music industries for distributing pirated versions of copyrighted materials. Beware viruses too, since file-sharing networks are a means of spreading these and other malware.
Copy broadcasts from a television using a DVD recorder or hard drive.	This falls under the fair-use exception to copyright if the purpose of copying the content is time-shifting (i.e. to consume the content at a time of the consumer's choosing).

Activity 16

One example is of course copyright law, which is aimed at deterring people from making unauthorised copies of digital content. This constrains people's online behaviour.

Activity 22

I thought of DRM, which aims to enforce copyright legislation.

Glossary

analogue hole   The fact that any audio signal in digital form has to be converted into an analogue form before it can be heard by the listener. Thus schemes to protect digital audio can always be circumvented by intercepting the audio signal once it has been converted into an analogue form.

content scrambling system (CSS)   A system introduced in 1996 to protect pre-recorded commercially produced DVDs from unauthorised copying.

copynorms   The social norms regarding the copying, distribution and use of created works.

copyright   A legal protection that guarantees that creators of content are rewarded for their work and protects the rights of users.

design rights   An area of intellectual property that applies to the physical appearance of an item or part of an item.

digital rights management (DRM)   A range of technologies used by copyright owners to control how the content they produce is used.

digital supply chain   A description of how digital content is created, processed and used, and how it gets from the creator to the consumer via a number of intermediate processes and intermediaries.

digital watermark   Data for the purpose of establishing authenticity that is embedded into digital content such as a graphic or sound file. The watermark is hidden, but can be revealed by running a program that can find it.

disc key   In DVD encryption, a key that is stored on the DVD itself and that is used to decode content that is encoded using the content scrambling system.

disc key hash   An encrypted version of the disc key that is stored on a DVD.

disintermediation   The trend towards a reduced role for intermediaries between creators and consumers, for example by consumers buying their music direct from an artist rather than from a record label.

fragile watermark   A digital watermark that does not survive transformations of the file in which the watermark is hidden. Fragile watermarks are used to indicate modification of the file.

HackSDMI   A challenge set by the SDMI Consortium to see if SDMI could be broken.

Intellectual Property Office (IPO) A government body that deals with intellectual property on behalf of the UK government. It is the office to which people submit patents and trademarks for approval.

intellectual property rights (IPR) The law relating to ownership of ideas, writing and other works of the mind.

patent A form of protection that gives the creator of a piece of work exclusive rights to use, produce and sell the work for a limited period of time in exchange for the creator making public the design and workings of the item.

piracy In the context of copyright issues, the illegal duplication of materials that are protected by intellectual property law.

player key In DVD encryption, a key that is embedded in a DVD player and that is used to decode content that is encoded using the content scrambling system.

robust watermark A digital watermark that is designed to survive common transformations such as compression or decompression of the file in which the watermark is hidden.

Secure Digital Music Initiative (SDMI) An initiative to form technical solutions to protect all parts of the music market, including the hardware for playing and recording music and the recordings themselves.

social norms The conventions by which societies operate, used to identify appropriate and inappropriate behaviours, attitudes, values and beliefs.

socio-technical system A system that involves the interaction of both people and technology in ways that are difficult or inappropriate to separate.

stakeholder A person or organisation that has an interest or concern in a particular operation, such as a business.

time-shifting Recording a television programme in order to watch it at a time of your choice. This is permitted by copyright law since it comes under the heading of 'fair use'.

title key In DVD encryption, a key that is used to encrypt an individual piece of work on a DVD. The title key is encrypted with the disc key and hence can be decrypted, and then used to decrypt the content of the piece, once the disc key has been found by the DVD player.

trademark A particular word or phrase and/or artwork that distinguishes a company's goods and services.

References

Anderson, C. (2007) 'Give away the music and sell the show', post on his blog *The Long Tail*, 28 January, http://www.longtail.com/the_long_tail/2007/01/give_away_the_m.html (accessed 8 May 2011).

Anderson, C. (2009) *Free: The Future of a Radical Price*, New York, Random House Books.

BBC (2006) 'Digital film: Industry answers', *BBC News* [online], 9 February, http://news.bbc.co.uk/1/hi/entertainment/4691232.stm#7 (accessed 11 April 2011).

BBC (2010) 'The BBC's approach to combating online piracy', post on *BBC Internet Blog*, 6 July, http://www.bbc.co.uk/blogs/bbcinternet/2010/07/the_bbcs_approach_to_combating.html (accessed 11 April 2011).

BPI (2010) *Digital Music Nation 2010*, London, BPI (British Recorded Music Industry) Ltd.

CNN (2003) 'CNN talks to Steve Jobs about iTunes', *CNN Tech* [online], 27 November, http://articles.cnn.com/2003-04-29/tech/jobs.interview_1_music-service-music-store-song-swapping-services?_s=PM:TECH (accessed 8 May 2011).

Corrigan, R. and Rogers, M. (2005) 'The economics of copyright', *World Economics*, vol. 6, no. 3, pp. 153–74.

Department of Transport (2010) *THINK! Road Safety* [online], http://www.facebook.com/note.php?note_id=55634820886 (accessed 8 May 2011).

Doctorow, C. (2007) 'Copy killers', *The Guardian* [online], 31 July, http://www.guardian.co.uk/technology/2007/jul/31/comment.drm (accessed 11 April 2011).

Gladwell, M. (2009) 'Priced to sell', *The New Yorker* [online], 6 July, http://www.newyorker.com/arts/critics/books/2009/07/06/090706crbo_books_gladwell#ixzz0xcL0xv4x (accessed 11 April 2011).

Hilton III, J. and Wiley, D. (2010) 'The Short-Term Influence of Free Digital Versions of Books on Print Sales', *Journal of Electronic Publishing* [online], vol. 13, no. 1, http://hdl.handle.net/2027/spo.3336451.0013.101 (accessed 8 May 2011).

IFPI (2010) *IFPI Digital Music Report 2010*, International Federation of the Phonographic Industry; also available online at http://www.ifpi.org/content/library/DMR2010.pdf (accessed 11 April 2011).

Jobs, S. (2007) *Thoughts on Music* [online], http://www.apple.com/uk/hotnews/thoughtsonmusic/ (accessed 11 April 2011).

Johnson, B. (2009) 'Does YouTube actually make any money?', *The Guardian* [online], 9 April, http://www.guardian.co.uk/technology/2009/apr/09/youtube-google-money (accessed 11 April 2011).

Kling, A. (2002) *Science and Markets* [online], http://econlog.econlib.org/GQE/gqe001.html (accessed 11 April 2011).

Lessig, L. (1999) *Code and Other Laws of Cyberspace*, New York, Basic Books.

McAlaney, J., Bewick, B.M. and Bauerle, J. (2010) *Social Norms Guidebook: A Guide to Implementing the Social Norms Approach in the UK*, West Yorkshire, UK, University of Bradford, University of Leeds, Department of Health; also available online at http://www.normativebeliefs.org.uk/ (accessed 11 April 2011).

Oberholzer-Gee, F. and Strumpf, K. (2010) 'File-Sharing and Copyright' in Lerner, J. and Stern, S. (eds) *Innovation Policy and the Economy, Volume 10*, University of Chicago Press.

Preston, B. (2010) 'Editorial', *Radio Times*, 4–10 September 2010.

Rosenblatt, B. (2010a) 'The ROI of RIAA Lawsuits', entry on his *Copyright and Technology* blog, 15 July, http://copyrightandtechnology.com/2010/07/15/the-roi-of-riaa-lawsuits/ (accessed 11 April 2011).

Rosenblatt, B. (2010b) 'Video Fingerprinting Gains Momentum for Contextual Advertising', entry on his *Copyright and Technology* blog, 3 September, http://copyrightandtechnology.com/2010/09/03/video-fingerprinting-gains-momentum-for-contextual-advertising/ (accessed 11 April 2011).

SABIP (2009) *Copycats? Digital Consumers in the Online Age* [online], Strategic Advisory Board for Intellectual Property Policy, http://www.ipo.gov.uk/ipresearch-copycats-200905.pdf (accessed 11 April 2011).

Sahi, S. and Felton, E. (2010) *Census of Files Available via BitTorrent* [online], http://www.freedom-to-tinker.com/blog/felten/census-files-available-bittorrent (accessed 11 April 2011).

Schultz, M.F. (2006) *Copynorms: Copyright and Social Norms* [online], Berkeley Center for Law and Technology, http://ssrn.com/abstract=933656 (accessed 11 April 2011).

Sousa, J.P. (1906) 'Machine Songs IV: The Menace of Mechanical Music', *Appleton's Magazine*, vol. 8, pp. 278–84; also available online at http://www.phonozoic.net/n0155.htm (accessed 11 April 2011).

Thompson, C. (2008) 'Clive Thompson on How T-Shirts Keep Online Content Free', *Wired Magazine* [online], vol. 16, no. 12, http://www.wired.com/techbiz/people/magazine/16-12/st_thompson (accessed 8 May 2011).

Umeh, J. (2007) *The World Beyond Digital Rights Management*, London, The British Computer Society.

Acknowledgements

Grateful acknowledgement is made to the following sources.

Tables
Table 1: © 'Twenty-Nine Ways to Acquire Content', CIBER Team. Crown copyright material is reproduced under Class Licence Number C01W0000065 with the permission of the Controller, Office of Public Sector Information (OPSI)

Figures
Figure 4: © Taken from www.learncenter.org

Figures 5 and 6: © Umeh, J.C. (2007) *The World Beyond Digital Rights Management*, The British Computer Society Publishing and Information Products

Figure 7: © Lessig, L. (1999) *Code and Other Laws of Cyberspace*, Basic Books

Part 5
Digital freedom: the good, the bad and the internet

Author: Paul Piwek

You can find this part of the block online. A link is provided on the TU100 website.